From Project-Based Learning
to Artistic Thinking

From Project-Based Learning to Artistic Thinking

Lessons Learned from Creating an UnHappy Meal

Raleigh Werberger

ROWMAN & LITTLEFIELD
Lanham • Boulder • New York • London

Published by Rowman & Littlefield
A wholly owned subsidiary of The Rowman & Littlefield Publishing Group, Inc.
4501 Forbes Boulevard, Suite 200, Lanham, Maryland 20706
www.rowman.com

Unit A, Whitacre Mews, 26-34 Stannary Street, London SE11 4AB

British Library Cataloguing in Publication Information Available

Library of Congress Cataloging-in-Publication Data

Names: Werberger, Raleigh, author.
Title: From project-based learning to artistic thinking : lessons learned from creating an unHappy
meal / Raleigh Werberger.
Description: Lanham, Maryland : Rowman & Littlefield, 2015. | Includes bibliographical references.
Identifiers: LCCN 2015034084| ISBN 9781475824599 (cloth : alk. paper) | ISBN 9781475824605
(pbk. : alk. paper) | ISBN 9781475824612 (electronic)
Subjects: LCSH: Project method in teaching. | Project method in teaching--Case studies. | Creative
teaching. | Creative teaching--Case studies.
Classification: LCC LB1027.43 .W47 2015 | DDC 371.3/6--dc23 LC record available at http://
lccn.loc.gov/2015034084

Printed in the United States of America

Contents

Acknowledgments

The author thanks the entire Darrow School class of 2018 for being willing guinea pigs. Their good humor and willingness to go along with what probably seemed like madness at the time made this project possible. Their enthusiasm carried me along when all I wanted to do was sleep. I also want to thank their parents for seeing the value of this project in what was billed as a history class, and their positive feedback helped me sustain me when I wondered if I had stepped in it.

In fact, the entire community of Darrow School contributed to our success. In particular, I want to thank Head of School Simon Holzapfel for supporting this project from the beginning, and Director of Studies Ingrid Gustavson, who helped me solve incredibly diverse problems, and talked me down from the ledge at times. Nikki Pressley, Caleb Corliss, and Craig Westcott helped me forestall disasters with their timely advice and interventions. Lily Corral was generous with her classroom, her time, and her knowledge. Dr. Ted Lightburn let me disrupt the Hands-to-Work program during his first year at the helm, and only rarely said "No."

So many people in the community contributed their time and their wisdom to help us. Schuyler and Colby Gail of Climbing Tree Farm in Stephentown, NY, gave the students hands-on opportunities to dig into farm work and understand why we were making these UnHappy Meals. Will at Four Fat Fowl let us into his inner chambers to see how he made his amazing triple-cream cheese. Paul Rix, Josh Coletto, and Rebecca Joyner worked with the students to help them figure out what they needed to do and how to do it.

Thomas Thwaites was influential in the conception of the project, and generous with his personal time. Beverly Naidus responded to a strange e-mail and helped me understand how art was a way of thinking that could be taught.

Finally, I thank my wife, Lindsay Foster, who took me with her to Germany and introduced me to an incredibly fertile world I hadn't understood before. She made me write when I didn't want to, and helped me figure out what I meant to say.

Introduction

This book is the record of an experiment to push the boundaries of student exploration and project-based work. It is a narrative about what happens when you teach history like an arts class, with a foundation in neuroscience and a healthy dose of existential philosophy. It is an exercise in skirting the line between improvisation and chaos in order to provide the most personalized education possible for students who didn't quite know what that meant. Nor, for that matter, did their teacher.

Ultimately, it is meant to resolve a series of questions that every teacher in a student-led classroom wrestles with:

- How does one teach how things work in the real world?
- How clear must a student (or a teacher) be about one's intent when undertaking a project?
- How does one transition students from passive receivers of knowledge to active learners?
- Where is the line between teacher direction and student freedom?
- How does one make students see a practical legacy, and a lasting value, for their work?

And of course, to solve this problem:

> Imagine you are stranded on an island, with no hope of rescue in the foreseeable future. You walk around the island, taking stock of your resources. You have a natural spring. You notice some wild vegetables and grains, and even a few shrubs growing berries that look suspiciously edible. Improbably enough, you also notice a small flock of chickens.
>
> You have enough to survive on, even long-term, before someone finds you. But you have not solved your biggest problem.
>
> How are you going to make yourself lunch?

Whatever else you learn from school, how can this not be the most important?

THE PURPOSE OF THIS BOOK

Progressive education is, at its heart, an attempt to recreate the actual conditions of learning by placing the students at the center. The teacher's job is not to establish what should or not be known, or to be the final arbiter to judge whether the student succeeded. The argument is that the more control the student has over content, creation, and assessment, the more authentic that learning is.

This places teachers in a classic double bind. The first challenge they must negotiate is finding that fine line between providing structure in the classroom and granting the students the freedom to learn as they should. Traditionalists argue that the progressive classroom is a place of chaos and frequent transgressions, and progressives argue that traditional classrooms are those in which students either sleep at their desks or constantly try to escape altogether. The truth is that progressive techniques cannot exist without boundaries or without some sort of routinization to practice skills.

The second trap is that modern education is split into several different disciplines, each with its own jargon and canon, each professionalized, and with its own set of standards. These disciplines are subsequently taught to K-12 students as inherently different modes of thought, and thus the typical middle or high school student wanders through the school day thinking science is one thing and history another, while poetry is read in this room and circles measured in that one. This ignores the fact that children don't learn this way before they go to school, and that people in the professional world are perfectly capable of being poets *and* scientists.

Or of writing poetry about science.

Progressive schools counter these problems by devising multidisciplinary projects that mimic the hands-on way children develop knowledge about the world. They try to make what is learned useful and applicable to the world. They find ways to allow the students the freedom to be self-expressive within the project, to have some control over what is built and how it is assessed. A cursory online search can pull up any number of studies that show the efficacy of this approach for raising student motivation and test scores.

Thanks to their belief in open sharing, these schools are willing to place student work on their websites, along with teachers' lesson plans and assessments. In a sense, both the students and teachers thus have authentic audiences for their work—that a need in the educational community for models of progressive practice is being addressed. A quick comparison of these examples reveals a series of requirements to make these sorts of projects work.

An artifact is designed that allows for both student originality but also for coverage of content and skills in a few different disciplines. Students might be instructed to take pictures of animals and plants and then find ways to illustrate principles of mathematics that occur in the natural world. Students might be instructed to develop a graphic novel depicting principles of economics, or create public service announcements about health crises affecting teenagers. They might be asked to build and then market, replate with business plans, an item that addresses ecological sustainability. Perhaps they could design the next killer app?

If the artifact is not set in stone, they might be given a design challenge, sent out into the neighborhood or on a virtual online tour to dream up solutions to actual problems in the community. The classroom then becomes the space for working out prototypes of these solutions. Ideally, the problems they need to solve and their solutions can be intertwined with the school's specific curricular goals. If the local folks need access to fresh vegetables, then the students should build a garden, and this becomes a natural way to learn biology and ecology.

Either way, these sorts of projects are reverse-engineered by teachers in planning sessions so that the necessary skills and content can be addressed, resources found, and benchmark stages developed. A tremendous amount of front-loading occurs before the students are ever introduced to the challenge. Formative assessments are designed to measure student progress and counteract any problems that may be developing. Schools that practice this form of education have redesigned their schedules and campuses—longer periods, combined classes, communal spaces, workshops, technology—to facilitate this kind of work. It is no light undertaking.

Once one starts to pull the loose threads of the modern American educational model this way—questioning classroom management, assessment, separated disciplines, homework—it's amazing how much becomes open to question. How can anyone be sure the students are as genuinely motivated by this style of learning as teachers think they are? Just how free and unique can student expression be within the structures that have been created to ensure quantifiable, means-tested success?

What might happen, for instance, if an experiment was devised that was ostensibly a design challenge, a project-based curriculum that actually violated many of the procedures around which project-based learning was organized? What if a test could be devised to see just how much teacher direction was needed to keep students on track, or how much individual freedom a student could be given in the interest of replicating the often random and self-directed way knowledge is accumulated by children?

Perhaps the greatest opportunities for driving student engagement and growth might come from forsaking clever but complicated projects and instead giving students simple challenges that hide infinite complexity and infinite choices. This would not happen at a school that had a daily schedule or student course load designed to support project-based learning, nor would it involve students who had had those kinds of experiences. What the school did have, however, was a commitment to hands-on work of a more traditional kind—in farming, sugaring, trail clearing, and woodchopping.

To raise the bar on the challenge, the teacher would develop a project idea for which he had no practical experience and no real sense for what the final product would look like. What the teacher did have was a hypothesis.

Every project that tried to maximize student creativity and voice incorporated the arts as a medium of communication. The arts are a critically rigorous way of coming to knowledge about the world. It relies on the body's senses for information. It asks questions like every other subject. It requires long hours of practice to develop its skills. It already embodies the idea that there are many different ways to express ideas. Why not just create an arts class that incorporated everything else into it?

The premise of the experiment is that teaching any class like a course in design in which every student should consider himself or herself, first and foremost, an artist, would marry the best aspects of project-based learning with the freedom, spontaneity, and self-discovery possible in the best arts classes.

Mr. Werberger's Teacher Journal

I gave my students a simple challenge: re-create the most iconic piece of global consumption—the McDonald's Happy Meal—by hand, using just the materials that lay around us.

That question launched a terrifying and joyous eight-month experience. Our aim was to show that we did not just learn to make a Happy Meal—rather that this "Unhappy Meal" revealed the way our world really works.

We mean to lure you, the reader, into hearing our story, which is really at the center of the way we all learn. I cast myself as a learner first, and we all worked together on the problem of how not just to make this food, but how to give it meaning, and then how to tell you about it.

We began by looking at the different ways families around the world feed themselves, then we swerved into an examination of imperialism at the turn of the twentieth century. We uncovered the consequences of our consumption (and the disposal of our trash) and began to see how each of our actions tied into a global web of dependencies and repercussions. Some delved into twentieth-century dystopias—Nazi Germany, Soviet Russia—while others examined the possible dystopias in our future.

We raised and killed chickens; we grew our own crops; we made our own paper and ink—sometimes from the strangest of sources. We learned how to find the resources we needed to make this possible. We taught each other how to see, how to think, how to write, how to create, and worked hard to make each other and ourselves better. We learned about ourselves, ultimately.

In the end, we had a radically different understanding of the way the world works and of our place within it. This journey was profound enough that we want to tell you how it all happened and what we discovered about the way we are meant to learn.

WHAT THIS BOOK CAN DO FOR YOU

You may be interested in project-based learning and hope to see a step-by-step account of what it looks like in the classroom, "live" over the course of a year. You may be familiar with it, or an experienced practitioner excited by its possibilities, but frustrated by its limitations.

You may simply be looking for a chance to reevaluate your own teaching style, hoping to add more creativity to your students' work.

You may want to see what student work looks like in this type of classroom, or learn what the students themselves say about it.

You may be curious about what it's like to work with students who are unfamiliar with the building blocks of project-based learning (PBL)—self-assessment, critical reflection, collaborative work—and want to slowly introduce them to the skills necessary to become a life-long independent learner.

You may be a teacher who wants to change your own classroom without having to change the entire school around you.

You may be a school leader who is curious about the kind of support your more adventuresome teachers might need to be successful in doing that.

You may be thinking about teaching your subject discipline as a professional discipline—as an historian practices history, or a scientist science.

You may want to find real-life, authentic projects to raise the stakes on your students' projects and to reach wider audiences.

You may be curious about how to bring professionals from the community into your classroom.

You may want to know what can go wrong with project-based learning (this, like every project, was not a 100 percent "success story") and how students and teachers deal with failure.

This book is *not* meant to be an abstract discussion on pedagogy, but a detailed narrative of an attempt to push progressive pedagogy to one logical conclusion.

HOW THIS BOOK IS CONCEPTUALIZED

It is difficult to write a book about a specific experience without having it read like a journal. It is perhaps better to treat it as the record of an experiment. Each chapter begins with a problem that teachers have to wrestle with—how to help students come up with questions or work together meaningfully. The thesis of the chapter is that an artistic approach to thinking can provide solutions to that problem. Throughout the book, each stage of artistic thinking will be defined—the conceptual tools of the artist, the practice of deconstruction, the guiding process of inquiry and investigation, creation, reflection, self-assessment, and exhibit.

The experiment that tested that hypothesis is then described. In each chapter, the students are given a challenge, and the narrative records how that challenge was implemented with respect to that corresponding step in the artistic process. Because every experiment requires raw data, excerpts from the teacher's journal will be included when it's important to understand his decisions, and what he saw unfold from them. Because no one wants purely raw data in the records of an experiment, the rest of the narrative is an attempt to explain classroom events in light of both progressive pedagogy and artistic practice.

Finally, this book addresses one of the bigger challenges teacher's face in using other classrooms as models for their own practice. While the final artifacts that students create are often available online, what is normally missing is a record of the students' thoughts while they are creating their work. Therefore, included as raw data are excerpts from the students' journals, and in some cases, the formative assessments they created as a way to assess their progress. Their words are also necessary to assess the validity of the hypothesis that forms the center of this book, since the food they created is long gone.

HOW THIS BOOK IS ORGANIZED

The first three chapters make the case for establishing artistic thinking as a fundamentally sound approach to teaching nonarts classes. The arts inject freedom of inquiry and student passion into a design thinking process that is itself already a deeper form of learning. Art is social, communicative, and focused on critical analysis, just as other disciplines are, but unlike the others (at least on a K-12 level) it is intensely personal, creative, empathic, and focused on challenging an audience, rather than placating it.

Much like other subjects, art teaches students how to focus on small details, how to fit small details into a larger pattern, how to ask questions, and how to carry out experiments to answer those questions. Therefore, the habits of mind practiced in an arts class transfer easily to other disciplines, but have the extra value of being crafts-based; that is, students are challenged to make something original and unique that represents their personal beliefs and passions.

Chapters 2 and 3 discuss how to create the environment for learning and making, for the habits of mind necessary for success for either art or science. The students will have to understand that learning is a social activity but it still requires space for quiet introspection. They will begin to develop their artistic tools: the ability to see with fresh eyes, the ability to think about what they are seeing, and the ability to ask questions that lead to exploration.

Creation is an act of engagement. It begins with a perception of the world and challenges it in some way. The creator perceives something uniquely individual, and strives to make that unique understanding visible to others. This should be as free as possible, allowing for surprise, for discovery, for trips, stumbles, and falls, to being able to leave work for a while and come back to it. The first third of the book is thus a preparation for the journey,

Chapters 4, 5, and 6 begin the actual project. In chapter 4 the students meet a Happy Meal for "the first time," and are challenged to deconstruct it. They are introduced to two different ways to practice design thinking. One will be based on the engineering design cycle—in which we take something apart and learn how to put it together again. This will be the UnHappy Meal, and their challenge is to provide a lunch that imitates the form of this most ubiquitous of all fast food meals. They must understand every component and how to make it.

Yet there will also be the artistic side of this challenge, in which this dissection will lead them to think more deeply about consumption, about health, about human social organization, and about the earth itself. These explorations evolve because they can see the smaller pieces, the deeper questions that begin to hit at existence and why things are they way they are. They will be asked not to remake, but to recreate, and to find self-expression in that act of re-creation.

Once they have learned to deconstruct objects they can begin to deconstruct themselves. Art is a journey to know oneself better in relation to the world. They will discover arts-based research. They will be reflective about the choices they make in their own explorations. They will ponder why some approaches become dead ends and others bear fruit. They will begin to understand how they learn.

Finally, the work of re-creation begins. The students will revisit the notion that learning is social, and they will re-engage with the world beyond the school. They will find mentors and understand that everyone is a teacher. They will balance their intellectual work with handiwork. They begin from seeds, chicks, moldy berries, and old newspapers. They end up in a pile of dead chickens.

In the final third of the book, the students balance intellectual work and handiwork with "soulwork." They are introduced to the idea that they are artists and begin to consciously create work with deep meaning. They will cautiously embrace the idea of provocation. They will have to think about their audience and how to curate an experience that will be transformative.

At the end, the hypothesis is evaluated. Its success, and indeed the very notion of "success," are discussed. Lessons are learned, and considerations for the future put forward. After all, there is no finish line in either art or learning. There is only another step.

ONE

Why the Arts Matter in School

Until children go to school, they tend to learn by getting their hands dirty. They taste objects, they smash them, they throw them at each other. They play games with rules that adults find confusing—and those rules can change at a moment's notice. They live in a constant process of negotiation with the environment and the people in it.

Children are prone to moments of deep fascination and focus even as they are prone to bouts of boredom. They fight with each other as much as they create together. They spend mind-bogglingly long periods of time performing rote tasks over and again to no seeming purpose.

Play is in fact a way of getting to know and understand the physical world and how to live in human society. It is unavoidably messy. If one assumes that each of these inexplicable moments is in fact an attempt to carry out experiments, to follow questions, to pile knowledge on top of knowledge, then it appears that children are crafting an epistemology. It's enough to make one wonder why schools spend so much time trying to put an end to these behaviors in the name of proper learning.

Progressive education models try with varying success to get closer and closer to this model of learning. They design practical experiences in building artifacts to provide hands-on illustrations of academic concepts. They develop methods for helping children work together collaboratively. They put students into the community to make learning even more real and authentic. In a sense, progressive education has been one long rebellion against the existence of the schoolhouse itself.

What then would education look like if the schoolhouse were virtually dissolved? How close to the original conditions of learning can a teacher take a class without it descending into chaos? Begin with the urge to create and let us reenvision the classroom as an art studio. Embrace the alternating moments of deep focus, wild leaps of thought, and the occa-

1

sional fracas as indications that learning is happening as it was designed to naturally. Artistic thinking is not just an equally valid way of deciphering the world as math, science, or history. It may be the original model for the way humans learned long before schools existed.

THE ARGUMENT

This book is not a summary of the reasons why school has to change. This book is not a call for project-based learning (PBL) or any other version of that in general. This book assumes you likely agree that classrooms need to be more student-centered, based more on inquiry, and more experientially connected to real-world issues. John Dewey believed this 100 years ago, and it's no less true today. If anything, improvements in technology have made it more urgent than ever to teach students to engage with the world, and yet easier to accomplish.

Project-based learning is a method of instruction that encourages students to develop questions and construct projects that encapsulate in some way the results of their investigations. Much of PBL is collaborative, and students learn how to work together to design and build their constructions. Higher level PBL encourages students to use the real world beyond the school to develop their questions and find resources, including experts in the professional world who can be recruited to resolve design and execution problems.

As Dewey suggested, what better way to learn math than to study the sewer systems under New York City. Or as he might say today, to learn physics by building water purifiers for communities with difficulty in accessing clean water. Design thinking, which embraces many aspects of PBL, supersedes it in that the students design their own challenges based on their experiences in the living community, talking to the people who live there, and addressing their needs. Rather than the teacher telling them to work on the sewer systems, students would have come across that problem on their own, led by their noses.

The premise is that this work becomes more authentic to students who feel as though there is a real, practical need for the work, and who can see the applications of their studies to professional life. Moreover, the idea that the work will be judged by outsiders, and will have a genuine use, gives students more of a stake in their outcomes. PBL has become a key strategy in helping students develop what businesses call "twenty-first-century skills"—that is, creativity, adaptiveness, communication, and collaboration.

These are not solely twenty-first-century skills—these have been necessary for the entire span of human existence. But it does mean that a number of initiatives have begun, often funded with seed money from technological and global businesses to begin PBL programs and schools throughout the country.

As Will Richardson notes in *Why School?*, "A recent IBM survey of CEOs asked them to name the most crucial factor for future success, and their answers had nothing to do with state assessments, SAT scores, or even Advanced Placement tests. Instead, they cited creativity and 'managing the growing complexity of the world.'" [1]

Some of these new PBL and Design Thinking-oriented schools, such as San Diego's High Tech High, are more famous than others, but they are all engaged in pushing the boundaries of progressive education. Much of this growth has occurred in charter schools that can build a PBL program from scratch, as it is much harder to change a school's existing curriculum to project-based learning.

A caveat: my own experience has been in designing and teaching a project-based program in Honolulu at my own school, and then serving as a founding board member for a new project-based charter school called the School for Examining Essential Questions about Sustainability.

WHAT EXACTLY IS PBL?

What is the general format of PBL? Students begin projects with a very clear sense of the questions they want to answer and the product they want to build. Projects often begin by deconstructing an example of the product and conversation often centers on designing a better version. Benchmarks guide student efforts and keep them on task.

PBL features several rounds of self- and peer-critique and consequent refinement of the product. Curriculum is taught through the projects—the teachers' goal is to find a project that allows them to deliver required content and skills and still engage the kids.

You will see your students grow in confidence, critical faculties, and maturity from project-based learning. They will become more engaged with the world, whether it is analyzing global events or the governance of their own school. This book is not an argument for project-based learning. You'll quickly see how the students' work speaks for itself.

This is not to say that PBL is perfect, or that it is the only answer. For an inquisitive teacher, PBL raises even more profound questions about the most effective way to work with kids.

- If one's goal is to provide the most authentic learning experience for kids, does the classroom itself need to disappear?
- If the goal of PBL is to maximize student creativity, how much control over the curriculum should the student then have?
- Does the hierarchical structure of "school" as we know it inherently derail the greater goal of progressive education—creating indepen-

dent, inquisitive young people who are prepared to find their life's
bliss on their own?

THE AQUAPONICS PROJECT

As an example, consider the case of the ninth graders in the Mid-Pacific
Xploratory program in Honolulu, Hawai'i. The students were challenged
in their Humanities and STEM classes to design and build a portable
aqua-ponics kit and market it on the web. This project was intended to
fold in geometry, biology, literature, history, and design. It was also intended to give students an authentic buy-in: to address the issues of
water conservation on an island that was experiencing drought, and the
promise of actually starting a business. Could the students develop and
market a portable closed ecosystem in order to teach people about the
importance of sustainability?

The implementation of the project was modeled on the way small
successful start-ups operate in the business community. First, the students studied both global and local issues concerning overconsumption
and its consequences—ecosystem disruptions, resource scarcities, and
human conflict. They then visited aquaponics farms to understand aqua-
culture and deconstructed existing products and business pitches to develop rubrics for their classroom work.

Project teams developed roles based on real-world counterparts—that
is, "contractors" were responsible to delineating tasks and communicating with their "staffs" and with the teachers; "designers" worked on
developing models for the kits; "salesmen" developed social media and
other outreach materials. Teams held weekly meetings to find out how
much work had been finished and how much was left to be done. Students felt personally responsible for their teammates' success and were
unhappy if they felt they had let down their teams.

Students found mentors outside the school who correlated to their
project roles. Parents were eager to bring their work skills and experiences into our classroom—not to lecture the whole class, but to work
with their younger analogues. Construction engineers, local craftsmen,
and business and marketing specialists came to the classroom. Local businesses, from aquaponics farms to "maker spaces," volunteered their
space and time to help students design and build their kits.

For the students, reading novels or historical documents became exercises in examining the authors' uses of rhetoric and persuasion. Understanding narrative began to matter more as students realized they had to
craft a compelling message for their campaigns. As they realized the
importance of communication in the professional world, writing exercises became a common sense preparation for life, not a chore.

The STEM teachers reported the same results for math and science lessons. In other words, the students saw the adoption of classroom skills as an important step for their future success. This didn't happen immediately, but by the last third of the project timeline, their attitudes had shifted markedly from where they had started the year.

More remarkably, this project even changed how they used their free time. Students enrolled in online courses in either website development or business development. Their use of social media took on more significance and had a more authentic stake for them, as students began communicating with web journals and community organizations to expand their online presence and gain "endorsements" for their products.

Eventually, their work became polished enough that they attracted the interest of a few local entrepreneurs who volunteered not only to teach them business skills but to host a *Shark Tank*-like event and bankroll the winners. One team walked away with $1,500 in seed money.

And yet, here is the problem. As summer approached, the students talked excitedly about their business plans. Then they all went on vacation. The following year, without direct reinforcement in the classroom, the students' business plans fizzled out completely. The students were waiting for the teachers to tell them how to proceed. Without that, interest waned, self-motivation disappeared, and even the allure of cash rewards failed to stimulate them to continue.

The engineering design process was instrumental in guiding student work. The cycle was identical to the one used by NASA. Identify a problem or a question. Identify the criteria for success on the constraints that limited possibilities. Brainstorm solutions. Develop a prototype. Test and critique the prototype. Reevaluate and refine. Refine some more. Refine even more. And so on until somewhere down the line you have finished an artifact that comes as closely as you can to your goal.

Ultimately, this process worked well in that every group competed its project on time. However, it had also created a convergence among the students' outcomes. That is, all of their designs more or less seemed the same due to the constraints and the criteria of the project itself. A fish tank below, a grow bed above, and the use of gravity to have the water percolate through the gravel. Square sides, because it's hard to bend plexiglass.

The end, which was the aquaponics tank, had dictated the means — that is, all aspects of the process and even the nature of success. The only role creativity played was in making a design with easier parts to fit together, and coming up with a catchy team name and logo.

Mr. Werberger's Teacher Journal

> I was the humanities teacher in the aquaponics project. Clearly, we hadn't yet built a sense among the students that these businesses were more than a school project. I began to wonder just how much of the excitement over aquaponics was really just ours—that the students had gotten invested in the kits because of the possibility of "getting rich," or because they knew the alternative was going back to textbooks. The subject itself, perhaps was not so fun. I felt we had failed in getting the students so personally invested in the work they would continue on without a guiding hand.
>
> I believe that that students had indeed learned how to collaborate effectively in their production teams, and they had certainly managed to communicate with confidence—that they had the courage to make sales pitches in front of over a hundred local professionals was proof of that alone. We saw them grow in their ability to analyze their work and the work of their peers critically.
>
> But I believe the project had failed in the supreme test—stimulating creativity, self-motivation, and joy in the work.

Did having a predicated purpose for the project take away from the other goal of project-based learning—the discovery of individual passions and the ability to express oneself? Does requiring a project to have a practical end—the recognition that some need in the community exists and that the project can fill it—make PBL too prescriptive from the beginning?

How does having such an externally directed approach square with the belief that PBL maximizes student creativity and self-direction? Is there a way to take the best aspects of the engineering process—its insistence on deconstruction, inquiry, collaboration, reflection, and refinement—and find room for the students to make their own way through their own education? To explore the topics they personally find compelling and to come up with their own sense of what's important to know?

A MODEST PROPOSAL

There is a subject discipline that has been recognized to not only help students achieve high academic outcomes, but also maximize student creativity, confidence, and individual self-expression. This subject is also becoming highly valued in the business world. This subject is, naturally, the arts.

Artistic design thinking incorporates the best aspects of engineering design thinking— beginning any investigation with essential questions, taking existing models to see how they tick, and then building on what came before, critical reflection and endless refinement. It is also a uniquely individual approach and stresses the product less than the process.

Artistic thinking does not, however, mean merely including art in a project as a means of self-expression, as a component that accompanies a science experiment, a math function, or historical investigation. Rather, it is a way of engaging with the world, and it is, at its core, an epistemology of its own.

In a way, it represents a radical departure from the way much PBL is currently taught.

It is an endless and restless investigation that strives to reveal the unexpected, which balances the painstaking development of skills with happy accident and bouts of lateral thinking, in which a flash of insight can take years to develop thoroughly (if at all.) Failure is a hundred times more likely than success, and "success" is a thing that may not even be desirable or understood to the audience or the artist.

This book's proposal is that incorporating artistic thinking into every school curriculum is essential to answering these questions. Yet it is slowly becoming rare in our classrooms. This comes at a cost to our students, but also to our teachers.

THE ADVANTAGES OF AN EDUCATION IN THE ARTS

American educators have long known about the benefits of an arts education—since the transcendentalist movement, certainly. Arts education correlated with much of John Dewey's philosophy, centering as it did on play and exploration. Moreover, as he wrote (in one of his most frequently reposted quotes), "Art is the most effective mode of communications that exists." He grounded his idea of aesthetics in everyday experiences, which aligns with his educational belief that contextual learning is all.

In Burton, Horowitz, and Abeles's, "Learning in and through the Arts," the teachers of elementary and middle school children reported that students in art-rich classrooms had a greater ability to communicate, were more willing to be risktakers, and collaborated better (in addition to being better creative thinkers).[2] One might conclude, "Of course! That's what art teaches! But if schools aren't testing for these traits, what does it matter?"

The Arts Education Partnership has suggested that art disciplines help students improve on core curricular subjects. Music, for instance, can increase proficiency in math and reading, and seems to boost SAT verbal scores, especially for ESL students, while the visual arts apparently can improve general reading, writing, and critical interpretive skills. Its report is not a matter of guesswork, but was in fact based on rigorous analysis of over sixty studies that tracked student achievement in the arts and on standardized tests and school performance.[3]

As another example, a study by the Solomon R. Guggenheim Museum also found that third graders who took part in a special visiting artists program (called Learning Through Art [LTA]) in New York City improved in problem-solving skills such as "flexibility (the ability to revise or rethink one's plans when faced with challenges), connection of ends and aims (the ability to reflect on whether one's final work of art met the intended goals), and resource recognition (the ability to identify additional materials that could be applied to the completion of the project)."[4]

Secondly, the study showed that students in the program developed a greater facility with language and critical insight than their peers. The report concluded, "[S]tudents who participated in LTA were able to apply skills they learned in the program—specifically, using inquiry to decipher a work of art—to text."

The results for teachers are also interesting. Burton et al. found that teachers in arts-rich schools were more creative themselves, more innovative, and happier on their jobs. This may be related to the fact that arts-rich schools exhibited a very different culture from traditional schools—less hierarchical, less formal, with more opportunities for teacher voice, and much more support for students based on their individual needs.

Researchers also discovered that the status of arts-rich or nonarts-rich schools was not tied to socioeconomic status, but rather to school climate, years of study in the arts, and opportunities to engage in more than one arts subject.

THE ARTS IN DECLINE

Despite its well-attested effects on student learning, the story of the arts in US education is a mixed bag. In some states there has been a precipitous drop, while others have stayed more or less the same. It also varies widely by district in each state, and by discipline within the arts. In no case, however, is arts education on the rise. Music and visual arts classes, for instance, have remained more or less steady, while theater and dance have nearly disappeared from elementary schools, according to a 2012 study by the National Center for Education Statistics.

No one will be surprised that schools serving lower income students see a disproportionate decline in arts programs. The National Endowment of the Arts 2008 survey titled "Arts Education in America: What the Declines Mean for Arts Participation, 2008," revealed that only a quarter of black adults had received any arts education as students, representing a 50 percent shift downward over a thirty-year period, and the number is low for Hispanics as well. As expected, whiter, more affluent schools saw their course offerings remain steady.

However, there is another story that is obscured behind the data concerning the number of arts programs being funded throughout the states. Only 57 percent of high schools require students to take an arts course for graduation. And only 15 percent of high schools require more than one course at that. In other words, schools may post the numbers to indicate that art classes exist, but the degree to which students are served by them remains open to question.

The case of the Los Angeles Unified School District (LAUSD) is interesting. While the state received a block grant of $110,000,000 for arts education in 2009, that money was made flexible enough to address other school needs, and the state budget for arts education meanwhile plummeted. LAUSD has seen a drop in elementary arts education of 40 percent, meaning that over half of its students see no arts instruction, and that number rises to as many as three quarters of all middle school students. In 2012, the LAUSD voted to make arts education a part of the core curriculum and thus prohibited from further cuts.

However, as a 2012 article by KPCC entitled "LAUSD Schools Face Challenge of Making arts Part of the Core Curriculum," by Tami Abdollah and Ricky O'Bannon, suggests, the idea of "arts education" is beginning to blur. Rather than thinking of arts education as a "silo-ed" subject discipline, teachers are seeing arts becoming integrated into students' lives in interesting ways.

> Kids with less access to dance, studio art, and chorus in school have turned to graffiti art, makeup application YouTube videos, fan art, and manga outside of school.
>
> "Man, it's a free for all out there for young people," says longtime arts consultant Eric Booth. "I don't think there is a starving of the arts in the life of the young, but … that impulse mostly lives outside of our educational institutions."
>
> "There's a huge production going on right now with kids making their own videos, putting them on YouTube," says Kerry Freedman, a professor and head of art and design education at Northern Illinois University. "There's a huge amount of visual arts being made out there by undergraduates and high school kids that aren't discussed in school."
>
> And, says Freedman, these kids are creating informal groups outside of school that are "doing a lot of teaching and learning."

One answer to the question of how to get students more exposure to the arts might be to integrate them into existing courses. Much of PBL, for instance, incorporates an artistic element to every project, usually as a means of communicating the results of a student's investigation by creating a gripping exhibition. An example might be adding the creation of a music video to a critical dissection of a novel, or having students design a magazine to house their research in science or social studies. Does it work?

The article concludes:

> "I have seen some failures in those experiments, where the arts become a handmaiden to pep up boring curriculum," Booth says. "I remember seeing the dance of the fractions, in which kids perform the dance that accurately displays their mathematical understandings. It was a good

kinesthetic math lesson, but those kids were no more engaged or interested in dance at the end of it than they were at the beginning."
Freedman warns that arts integration has often led to "spotty" arts
instruction, with specialist teachers reduced or eliminated. Often,
Freedman adds, arts lose out to other subjects.
Steven McCarthy is the K-12 arts coordinator for LAUSD, and he teaches arts integration in the USC Master's of Education program. He says
he's a big advocate, but rather than replacing specific art classes, he
believes it should supplement what exists.
"But that isn't always possible in our economic climate," McCarthy
says. "So given a choice of no arts instruction and arts instruction
through integration, I'm going to take the integration."

So it seems there are two possibilities to increase the role the arts can play
in general education. One is to create student projects that incorporate
artistic disciplines. This does allow for more creativity and perhaps transference of art skills to other academic areas. However, this approach does
not necessarily answer the question of how to balance the arts with core
disciplines, nor does it completely resolve the question of how to create
opportunities for more open inquiry by students.

Another approach might be to stop thinking about the arts as *creative
skills or tools*, and instead, consider art as a *form of thinking*.

CREATING ART VS. THINKING ART

What is the difference between creating art and *thinking* art? Consider
engineering design for a moment. The aquaponics challenge began with a
question: Can students design and market a small, contained ecosystem?
The students brainstormed until they had a theoretical model, and then
they built and refined physical examples of that model until they had one
that met the challenge.

If engineering design leads to a product that answers an essential
question, the art process seems to lead to a deeper comprehension of the
question itself. An artistic investigation seeks to clarify the questioner's
relationship to the issue, and how to communicate that understanding.
Artists ask, "How does this affect me? How can I explain what I see to
others?"

The work that is created is an attempt to explore these questions, not
to answer them. Often, these questions are insoluble—evidence for which
we see, because artists continually change their styles and their tools in
response to these explorations. For that reason, some artists prefer to call
their work an "experiment" rather than a project.

Mr. Werberger's Teacher Journal

> Here's another way of putting it. My STEM partner during the aqua-
> ponics project used to say, "If you don't know where you're going, any
> road'll do." The point is that if students don't know what they're trying
> to accomplish, they will struggle to complete their work. It sounds
> obvious, but it's surprising how many class projects fail because the
> teacher fails to be clear enough about expectations, and the students
> aren't clear about what they need to make. This became our mantra
> through the year.
>
> When I recited this quote to my wife, a photo and video artist, she said,
> "That sounds really pleasant. I like getting lost." I had to explain to her
> that this was a negative thing. But the more I explained my under-
> standing of the quote, I started to think, "Well, sometimes I like getting
> lost, too."
>
> Maybe that should be happening more in school.

ART EMBRACES ACCIDENT

That's not to say there is not forethought, planning, or rigor in the creation of art. It features the same cycle of questioning, brainstorming, creation, and reification as the engineering process, but it embraces the occasional swerve, as well. If anything, it may even be more rigorous than
engineering, as an artist can't just throw out pieces that don't fit. That one
weird piece may be more important than the ones that were intended.

This is sort of different from practicality or mastery—it is pure exploration for its own sake. And this is interesting because so much of technological innovation has been accidental or secondary to the stated goal of
the activity. There is a fairly long list of game-changing technologies that
were discovered by accident, from corn flakes to microwaves to vulca-
nized rubber. Again, does having a practical purpose for a project elimi-
nate these happy accidents or detours? What if the detour is all?

The value for the student is the sense of delight that accompanies new
discoveries. As Elliot Eisner said in his John Dewey Lecture for 2002 at
Stanford University:

> In the arts, ends may follow means. One may act in the act may itself
> suggest ends, ends that did not see the act, but follow. In this process
> ends shift; the work yields clues that one pursues. In a sense, one sur-
> renders to what the working process suggests. . . . Uncertainty needs to
> have its proper place in the kinds of schools we create. How can the
> pursuit of surprise be promoted in a classroom?[5]

Again, this is not to suggest learning methodology is not important. Of
course it is—adherence to some sort of consensually valid process is critical to establishing one's credibility. But is there space for a project to take

a turn when it's necessary, to die, if necessary, in order to pick up a new thread that may be more powerful for the student? If a history class suddenly delves into quantum physics because the students find it fascinating, isn't it worth changing direction? The end of education is not to learn a specific topic, it's to become a fuller human being, and part of that is learning to follow one's curiosity.

How do we teach children to see new uses for everyday things, which Sir Ken Robinson refers to in his lecture *Changing Education Paradigms* as "the process of having original ideas that have value." In the 1960s, George Land and Beth Jarman carried out an experiment that is still widely cited among progressive educators. They tested three- to five-year-old children in what is termed divergent thinking—or the ability to come up with large numbers of solutions to a given problem. Ninety-eight percent of those kids tested at the level of "genius." Those same children were tested five years later, and the percentage of geniuses had fallen to 32 percent. This dropped to a mere 12 percent five years after that.[6]

The test they gave these children was adapted from tests NASA uses to find the most creative engineers. This is the test in which children under the age of six score overwhelmingly as geniuses. This is the same test, which adults fail miserably. What happens to this creativity over the course of a child's growth? Is a standardized, one-size-fits-all education system the culprit?

Art has the ability to make us perceive the commonplace in new ways that shake our belief in what we know. In other words, arts open up the myriad possibilities that get closed by our epistemology. The most creative and unexpected solution is not always the best or most useful, but if the goal is to expand the range of possibilities—and we call that "innovation"—it's another argument in favor of building an educational curriculum around the arts, not the other way around.

CRITICAL DESIGN

Thomas Thwaites, a graphic designer, appeared on both a TEDTalk conference and the Colbert Report to talk about his experiences in building a toaster from scratch—literally from ground zero. He was pondering a question raised in Douglas Adams's *Mostly Harmless*—whether a human from a technologically advanced society would in fact rule like a wizard-king over a more primitive society, or be so helpless, in fact, from an over reliance on modern consumer society on he'd be dead weight.

As he put it, he was provoked by the line, "Left to his own devices he couldn't build a toaster. He could just about make a sandwich, and that was it." He decided to see if that was true.

He began by taking a toaster apart to see what he needed to make. He said that in general, the deconstruction of a model at the beginning of the project is meant to provoke questions down to the minutest detail. The more closely you look at something, no matter how familiar, the stranger it gets. The standard toaster becomes a wonder of engineering and holds multitudes of parts that seem to not only defy explanation, but which are aesthetically beautiful by themselves. Children seem to deconstruct objects around them almost instinctively. What some call "destruction" others may call "learning."

His book, *The Toaster Project*, collects the documentation he made along the way—traveling back and forth across Great Britain in search of minerals to smelt the metal for the wires and case, finding oil to make the plastic, e-mailing experts and engineers, and so on. He says that *that* is the art—not the toaster. The story of his journey is the project. The process is the goal. "It's not about actually making the toaster, it's following where the process of making the toaster takes you, and talking to people as you go." Unexpected roads sometimes yield the most profound experiences.

Moreover, that journey also functioned as the exhibit itself. As Thwaites says, "The beauty of the conversations you have is that you sort of make the experts think more fundamentally about what they know. By being an artist, you are talking to people from a different perspective—an outsider—which not only gives you access, but which can even make the experts reevaluate how they think."

As Thwaites tells it, British Petroleum's Public Relations liaison had no decipherable response to his request to order a pail of raw crude oil in order to make plastic. Moreover, he exhausted the capacity of an expert at the Royal School Mines to help him smelt a small amount of steel. Thwaites was reduced to using a medieval manuscript and Stone Age tools to replicate twentieth century technology. Again—deconstruction leads to unfamiliarity when theoretical knowledge is tested in the physical presence of an object.

Various disciplines entered into the project, making him think about things he hadn't planned on ever having to consider learning about such as metallurgy, for one, or considering the global economy or deep ecology. Moreover, he noted that our modern production processes are useful for making large complicated objects, while making small simple things required him to use ancient technologies—and to go to medieval libraries for this knowledge.

By the end, Thwaites challenges his audience to think about why something so amazingly complicated to create costs so little at the store. And who bears the true cost of our modern lifestyle—in terms of pollution, resource scarcity, low wages, the destruction of wildlife, and so on.

In other words, the exhibit is not just proudly showing your work—it is actually where the real conversation begins. It is the catalyst for a new round of the investigation, but one that involves the public. It gives people the space to think about things for themselves and leads to new actions and explorations. As he says, the danger in activism is in bludgeoning people over the head about how horrible everything has become and how we all just need to change *now*. People will not change, not all at once and not in the way you want. You have to work with people where they are.

This is the beauty of what he calls "critical" or "discursive" design: the product at the end of the process of artistic creation is a chance for the creator to provoke the audience to recognize an issue that most may not even realize exists (or which may in fact only exist within the artist) but which is fundamentally designed to alter one's perception of the world. This is one purpose of art, no—to make the viewer see things in a new way?

As he wrote on his website, Thomasthwaites.com, as of July 10, 2014, "So, I am a designer, but in the broadest sense of the word I suppose. I guess design is becoming broader and broader and that's something, which I'm kind of pleased about! I'm coming from this area of design which was variously being called critical design or speculative design, or discursive design—the idea of which is to use methods and techniques and processes, tricks of design, not to necessarily make products for sale, but to investigate the world around us and then to present these investigations, to society at large."

What might it look like to spend a school year, or a series of years, building from one project to the next, always linking a past investigation to a new one, using past insights to develop further insights? Our brains don't like disjunctures—arbitrarily jumping from one subject to the next without a bridge. We naturally build stories to link our knowledge so that we can understand it. A natural course of study would perhaps play to that strength. In that case, could arts education be that critical component—a way of linking all the disciplines and replacing the scattershot schedule and disciplinary compartmentalization we currently experience in schools?

Perhaps critical design—making projects that speak deeply to the student's passions and concerns, and which can also provoke an audience in both the best and worst ways during the exhibit—could provide the springboard to fulfill what every school mission statement claims to create in its students:

- a lifelong commitment to learning
- an engagement with the world
- an aesthetic appreciation for beauty
- the capacity for reflection, self-expression, and critical thought

WHAT IS THE VALUE OF STUDENT WORK?

Reflective teachers ask themselves some basic questions when they assign work or assessments:

- What is the usefulness of this for the student?
- What is its purpose?
- Is this necessary?
- What is the learning that is being assessed and what type of feedback should I give?
- Do the students understand my expectations and how to meet them?

Those who go deeper also ask: Will students be able to improve this? Should they be able to? Should I be the one assessing it?

The deepest question of all should be: Will they love what they have created? Where will this go when it's done? Will it make the world a better or a more beautiful place?

Mr. Werberger's Teacher Journal

> We thought we made significant steps in addressing the second set of questions when we asked students to provide peer and self-critiques on project benchmarks or major assessments and return to their work to improve it based on those critiques. And moreover, when we asked students to create a portfolio of assignments that reflected their growth and continuing challenges.
>
> Yet I wonder where those portfolios are now . . . back in the landfill? Or permanently deleted? We missed the last series of questions even though out entire project was based on hitting that level.
>
> Curiously, I have seen students (and teachers) hang on to art for years. Part of that may be pride, but I expect not a little of that has to do with the little piece of your soul that goes into that work. Or even more so, what that piece had to do with how you felt when you made it. Hopefully, that artwork was only a step on the way to a longer journey—not the end of it.

Art stems from an individual engagement with the world. The purpose of art is not to learn to use a set of tools (the camera, the brush, one's own body). It is to use the tools to explore something that is personally important to the artist. Moreover, artists seek to change the way they use those basic tools, to supersede limitations that muddle their message.

That is vastly different than, say, a history or a math class for the vast majority of students who encounter those subjects in school. Apart from the occasional historian or mathematician who emerges from high school, most students learn a basic set of skills, apply it to a given problem, and rarely adapt those skills to make meaning of the world outside of the school. What other message should a student receive after an entire childhood spent being tested on content knowledge to measure their academic success?

The artistic process is about clarifying a question, not answering it. It is a process of experimentation, not necessarily resolution. The artist is never finished. There is never truly a "final product." There is no "end," only more questions. If anything, the finished piece of art will likely either provoke an artist to go deeper into the question, or to shift entirely into a new direction. This is why we like seeing an artist's entire body of work—not just the last piece. We want to see the artist evolving and changing.

What does the artist want? Well, to shock you. If not to shock you, then at least to shake you. The artist wants to call your attention to something, to make you rethink your convictions, to contemplate a new way of seeing things. Art that reassures you is called "kitsch," and it's the stuff you find in doctor's waiting rooms or hotel lobbies. Artists exhibit work not to show off, but because they are trying to tell you something.

Can something similar be said about a student's project exhibit? It's important for students to know they have to stand publicly behind their work, yes, but what can turn the exhibit from the thought "My, what nice work the students have made," to "My, I never thought of that before, at least in that way, and I would like to know more"?

What work can students do—which still has deadlines, and peer critique, and multiple iterations, and content knowledge and skills—that promotes creativity and self-expression *and* critical reflection and thought?

Mr. Werberger's Teacher Journal

How do you teach students to think artistically?

I spent a year with my wife in Germany during her arts residency. Her program brought artists of all disciplines from all over the world to live together in a small palace (or *Schloss*) in Stuttgart. In addition to the visual or performing artists, some were philosophers, some were architects, some were engineers. I learned quite a bit about the nature of their experiments, but I was more curious to learn why they had become artists, and how they had learned to do what they did. I met with twenty of them and asked them a series of questions by way of investigating this phenomenon.

I asked them first which tools or abilities an artist needs. All agreed that being willing to take risks, questioning everything, and thinking and reflecting critically were mandatory. Others insisted effort mattered—being willing and able to follow a tiny lead to something else, or repeating your efforts time and again until you get skilled at communicating your ideas.

You must have desires and dreams, and be prepared to make discoveries, rather than being fed what you need. You figure out your interest by deconstructing some things in order to make others.

Intuition mattered, of course, as discovery isn't necessarily logical. Rarely does one jump from a point to the next connected one. Connections can be discontinuous, if that makes sense. As one of the artists said, "Try to make a conversation between a person's notebook and her glasses!"

Incidentally, many of the methods that they suggested are features of project-based or challenge-based education. Every project should begin with asking questions to invest the students in the investigation. As PBL teachers, we had worked hard to find ways for the students to engage with their own interests and passions. And we had incorporated as many opportunities as we could for the students to reflect on their thinking and perform constant iterations of their work. We stressed that there is no such thing as failure in their work—there was only a process of continual refinement. Yet we saw these as tools to make the work better—not as ends in and of themselves.

Second, I asked the group if there was a moment when school has taught them these tools or skills.

The most common response? "Depends on who your art teacher was."

One mentioned a teacher who refused to allow yes/no answers, while another said she had been allowed to use Alternative methods of presentation, such as a video installation. Sometimes there was a single moment that crystallized things, as when a teacher once asked, "Please draw me a beautiful picture" without any other instructions, while others mentioned getting constant positive affirmation.

A few said they passed through school in a daze, as there was nothing project-based, nothing open-ended, nothing artistic to engage them. And intriguingly, one person recounted how she surmounted the lack of resources at her school by means of a self-organized group of students who met independently to create art.

What's striking is how often many of these artists had a moment in their high school experience that opened up the doors to being an artist for them. I was actually imagining that they would have much more negative memories of their education. That said, most of those positive experiences happened either in art classes—or even despite the school, as they were able to build like-minded communities of students to support each other outside the classroom.

The third and final question was how to make schools the places where artistic thinking could be taught. I am writing their responses here verbatim:

- "Support students' explorations of their own interests and fantasies. Allow 'nonscholarly' interests. Have the class follow a student's interest (not the teachers'). Or, at least develop the curriculum together with the students."

- "Find teachers who can give everyone attention, nurture them, encourage them."
- "Have interdisciplinary conversations. And within disciplines, question the form, that is, how history is taught, not just focusing on historical details."
- "Understand that every question is valid."
- "Tell stories, especially about failure."
- "Allowing nonlinear paths to solutions. There are no right or simple answers."
- "Have more self-directed study and a looser curriculum."
- "The teacher doesn't have to know everything."
- "Create a safe environment. Establish a room or space that functions differently from the rest of the school. Develop respect within/ among the students."
- "Break apart the traditional roles of students and teachers, have them work together or so nonscholarly activities together. Get teachers to discuss their own interests and hopes."
- "Don't occupy every moment with activities—allow for 'incidentality.'"
- "Teachers should be willing to learn from students."

If there is any commonality in these responses it's that thinking artistically is about following one's own interests and desires, and being able to draw many different kinds of conclusions from the world around you. That may mean making connections between objects that are not normally connected in our minds, or otherwise reimagining the nature of relationships in the world. It's heavily inquisitive of course, involving the asking of questions—but more important, questions that do not often have easy answers or even any answers.

The essential skill that students need to be successful in thinking creatively is being comfortable existing "in the dark." It's likely teenagers are already there, so imagine how comforting it might be if they knew we are all in that same space together, and it's okay.

Finally, take heart in the insistence that the traditional relationships between teachers and students have to be rethought. The best way to model learning is for the teacher to be a learner, and for students to become teachers. But more than that, they are suggesting that the teacher and the student must work together to develop not just relationships, but the curriculum and classroom themselves.

There were also hints in their responses that the classroom itself must be reimagined as a different kind of space—not the traditional place of organization and discipline and work in the older sense of learning, but a space in which imagination, creativity can be allowed full reign.

Ultimately, artistic thinking does not have to occur solely within our classes, but can be common instead to any subject within the traditional curriculum. One should as easily become an artist from algebra class as from an arts class. It is as much a matter of approach as it is of skill.

USE THE ARTS AS A FUNDAMENTAL APPROACH

Various schools and educators adopt PBL to varying degrees. Again, this means having multidisciplinary projects with real world applications (usually investigating a local issue to bring in community leaders); student-based instruction (in which students develop inquiries, self-identify needs and strategies, heavy use of peer and self-evaluation according to student-created rubrics); heavy use of web tools for communication and creation; the use of the engineering design process (designing with the end in mind, use of peer-critique, reiteration); and exhibit and presentations of learning.

Challenge-Based Learning (CBL) is similar but has a different goal. It creates an open-ended challenge that students have to fulfill. "How can we stop racism? How can we stop people from polluting? How can we make school a more powerful learning experience?" CBL offers more opportunity for kids to pursue their own answers, to develop their own challenges, inquiries, and projects over time (more so than PBL, which does however have the advantage of providing organization, scaffolding, resources, and a clearly delineated schedule along with an achievable goal, all worked out by the teachers beforehand).

Beyond integrating the arts into a project, then, perhaps thinking like an artist *first* can make learning more investigative, more creative, and even more open-ended in terms of results. What might this look like?

A good project should in some way require the kids to look more deeply at something they take for granted—something banal yet ubiquitous, and always overlooked, like a toaster.

The project should in some way require kids to rethink what they think they know and reevaluate their stance toward that object and what it represents.

The project should in some way lead to an exhibit that has the same function for the audience that the project did for them—it should *provoke* an audience, rather than *satisfying* it. The project should provide the opportunity to practice good aesthetic design.

The project should also, educationally, tie in different disciplines and offer "real-world" applications for what they are learning.

The project does not have to be the avenue to teach specific content according to standards—it can stand-alone and be a tie-in, but does not have to direct all the learning.

The project should not in fact be the real goal—the project is the means for the process. The process shall in fact inform the goal of the project, if that makes sense. The project should be flexible enough to change in midstream if need be, as the *process* is the place where enlightenment happens.

And the project should also help the students develop essential questions that are more in line with their own interests. Teachers develop essential questions to inform the direction of the project, and then design opportunities to make the essential question relevant to the kids. Perhaps this is backward, perhaps teachers should merely lay out the challenge, and let the project itself be the means by which the essential question becomes clear to the students. This may be a way to teach the kids how to develop their own questions and devise the means to investigate them—within the framework of the challenge.

Mr. Werberger's Teacher Journal

The Project Idea
So, what is the challenge? Something that is universal to the teenage experience, something that has opportunities to embed every subject within it, something that can touch upon any number of social moral issues, and something they can physically construct.

Consider the opening question again: You are stranded on an island, with no hope of rescue in the foreseeable future. You walk around the island, taking stock of your resources. You have a natural spring. You notice some wild vegetables and grains, and even a few shrubs growing berries that look suspiciously edible. Improbably enough, you have also noticed a small herd of cows. You have enough to survive on, even long-term, before someone finds you. But you have not solved your biggest problem. How on earth are you going to make a Happy Meal from all of that?

Well, can they? Can they make all the components of a typical Happy Meal, in the same way Thomas Thwaites built his toaster?

Logistically, this would entail breaking down the Happy Meal to its constituent parts, and then figuring out how to assemble the ingredients. It would involve growing the vegetables, making the cheese and ice cream, and then perhaps just visiting a few cows and visiting the killing floor rather than having to procure their own meat. Perhaps not threshing grain, but understanding how wheat evolved with human intervention, how to grind it into flour or meal, how to raise yeast colonies, even how to build a basic oven and bake their own bread.

During our conversation, Thwaites suggested they even make the box, the wrapping, and the toy, which would require an understanding of paper making, ink, plastic, marketing, and so on. The soda component raises questions as well.

We would have to find the experts who can help us make these things, we would have to get our hands on the basic resources, and we would have to consider the way these things are procured in the larger world so that we may have a proper basis for comparison for our own efforts.

In terms of the larger goal of the project, the essential questions that would arise from that investigation are seemingly endless—whether questioning industrial versus small farming, our relationship to the animals we eat, international trade and economies of scale, working conditions in the fast-food industry, questions about diet and health, and finally, how we ourselves are affected by the nature of the food industry and what we can do about the bits we don't like.

And one would think the exhibit would center on those essential questions (the burger itself is really about showmanship, isn't it?) and requiring the audience to consider their own feelings about those questions. Those questions would evolve from the project—from the process itself—which from what I'm learning is the basis of artistic inquiry. Finally, if the students know their work would become part of this book, that it would be seen by an audience larger than their teachers or their parents, would it have an affect on the stakes? Might they not learn something about the nature of publishing itself, of presenting an original idea to the widest audience possible?

NOTES

1. Will Richardson, *Why School?: How Education Must Change When Learning and Information Are Everywhere*, Kindle ed. (TED Conferences, September 10, 2012).

2. J. M. Burton, R. Horowitz, and H. Abeles, "Learning in and through the Arts: The Question of Transfer." *Studies in Art Education* 41, no. 3 (Spring, 2000): 228–257, doi: 10.2307/1320379.

3. Tamara Henry, "Study: Arts Education Has Academic Effect," *USA Today*, May 19, 2002, usatoday30.usatoday.com/news/education/2002-05-20-arts.htm.

4. "Guggenheim Study Reveals Importance of Arts Education in Development of Problem-Solving Skills and Creativity," Guggenheim Museum website, www.guggenheim.org/new-york/press-room/releases/3400-aps-release.

5. Elliot W. Eisner, "What Can Education Learn from the Arts about the Practice of Education," 2002, www.infed.org/biblio/eisner_arts_and_the_practice_of_edu cation.htm.

6. Bryan Goodwin and Kirsten Miller, "Research Says: Creativity Requires a Mix of Skills," *Creativity Now!*, vol. 70, no. 5 (February 2013): 80–81, 83.

TWO

How to Set the Stage

No one learns how to play sports theoretically, and the best way to learn to drive is to start behind the wheel (preferably in an empty parking lot), not by reading the car manual. It seems odd, therefore, to start a classroom by diving straight into content, without giving the students an understanding of what they should do with it. No one actually learns history from a textbook, just dates and names. "Doing" history means thinking historically. Similarly, if students are going to be asked to think like artists, they should start by exploring their tools.

HOW DOES ONE CREATE THE ENVIRONMENT FOR LEARNING?

What are the parameters a teacher can set on day one that will give students the freedom to discover what they want to know, but still give them the structure to be successful? A learning space should support and liberate at the same time. This is a conceptual space, not a physical one. We are going to be fully mobile, and we cannot always choose the concrete space in which we will learn. But we can address certain habits of mind. What should these be? Look to the arts for an answer.

Artists operate under some basic frameworks when they begin to create. They assess their tools—the means by which they will create—and what they are able to accomplish with them. They understand they are creating their work in a social context. They are in a dialogue with previous work, seeking a way to have a unique voice within that conversation yet be a part of it.

They are also engaged in the present—with people, surroundings, and events that inform their work. Finally, they are in conversation with the audience who will see the work, and who will co-create meaning along with them. These realities are understood from the beginning and form the process by which the artist creates.

Similarly, you can start by imagining the classroom. What are the basic assumptions going to be—the operating principles? What must students know from the very first day?

They must understand that learning begins with assessing what they know already, and learning to place new information in that context. They will also have to know to assess how much they have learned over time and how far they have traveled.

They must also understand that the class is going to be a social construct in which we all will learn from each other, and to do that we have to trust that process.

Finally, if we are going to create like artists, we must accept that our work is going to be publicly viewed and have a public purpose.

Once we understand these principles, we can begin to create.

SO YOU WANT TO BE AN ARTIST

How do you start? What is your first step?

> When I sit down to write or make a drawing, I don't always have a coherent idea in mind. Often it is an amorphous feeling, bound up in the tissues of my body, waiting anxiously for release. I put the stylus on the tablet and brush to paper, and something that needs to flows out. It could be a confused memory or some spirit moving through.[1]

> Creativity is paradoxical. To create, a person must have knowledge but forget the knowledge, must see unexpected connections in things but not have a mental disorder, must work hard but spend time doing nothing as information incubates, must create many ideas yet most of them are useless, must look at the same thing as everyone else, yet see something different, must desire success but embrace failure, must be persistent but not stubborn, and must listen to experts but know how to disregard them.[2]

Here's the challenge: study 100 different artists, and you will come to a hundred different conclusions about the artistic process. Compare this to the hundreds if not thousands of teaching manuals that purport to show you the single best way to manage your classroom, in five easy steps, in eight essential tasks, or in three incredibly effective techniques. If teaching is an art, it cannot be reduced to some simple equations to be repeated in any setting.

On the other hand, any artist must begin with the same step—visionary or not, one cannot create without an understanding of the tools.

Brush, paints, and canvas; clay and potter's wheel; focus, shutter, aperture, and the camera. You can't challenge tropes if you don't know how to make them first.

Picasso went through several genres and styles before he developed Cubism. "4:33" worked because John Cage had already explored so much of what music could be before he stumbled across silence.

What then must be the tools for ninth graders about to begin a project that will require them to be, in equal parts, crime scene investigators, foragers and tinkerers, stealth activists and archivists, with a streak of the street-artist provocateur?

- They must learn to think in terms of questions and wonderings, rather than in packaged answers.
- They must know how to deconstruct a model to find what's worthy of emulation, and what can be changed for the better.
- They must use these deconstructions to provide a framework—a rubric—to guide peer critique and self-evaluation.
- They must practice self-reflection to assess what has been learned, and what has yet to be.
- They must develop a critical eye—seeing what's there (and what's missing,) and comparing and contrasting the evidence to develop hypotheses about meaning.
- They must ask questions and investigate answers, to discover resources and evaluate their uses.
- They must get used to having a public audience for their work.
- They must become adaptive and stretch our resources in service to their interests.
- They must find a way to bring their own personal passions and skills to my class.

And most of them, unless they had gone to fairly progressive middle schools, would be starting from scratch. As in, ground zero.

Yet the reality was that they had a great deal of experience in using these tools in other settings. Students are used to using how-tos and social networks to learn how to play musical instruments and video games. Most people learn to play sports without much direct training from a paid professional. Players watch each other and then take risks in practicing what they see.

The typical classroom can be a place of great fear just as much as an ice rink can be for someone who has never skated before. Kids remorselessly judge each other at first sight, and the smallest mistakes can become the focus of teasing and other social pressures. Add to this that the teacher appears as the Great Evaluator, seemingly prepared to criticize any student errors, and some children will respond to this environment by refusing to engage whatsoever.

What mitigates the fear in risk taking somewhat is in having some firm ground to stand on. One way of processing all this new information is by attaching it to what is already known.

STARTING WITH WHAT YOU ALREADY KNOW

Artist and University of Washington, Tacoma, professor Beverly Naidus views creative expression as a human birthright to be *tapped* rather than *taught*. In her book *Arts for Change: Teaching Outside the Frame* she describes a project she developed for community activists with no real art training. At first she showed the students examples of socially engaged art, covering topics ranging from racism to militarism to ecological destruction. But then the real work of teaching (or facilitating, as she terms it) began:

> After the slide show, we would invite students to meet in small groups to share a social issue that affected them personally, on a gut level. . . . We encouraged students to think about the issues that affected them directly on a daily basis, rather than engaging only intellectually or superficially with a topic.
> One student was worried about the growing global disappearance of clean water. She didn't feel she was truly confronting that issue emotionally on a daily basis, but working on the topic was a good way to avoid dealing with more immediate problems. . . . We talked about a way that she could combine her more intellectual but still very valid concern, with the emotional ones that ruled her daily stress. . . . One way to describe this process is to say that it means working from the core, rather than from what you think you should be talking about in your art.

Naidus continues:

> Students would share their stories for about ten minutes each, without cross talk, listening carefully to each other. After every student had spoken, all were invited to discuss how the stories were connected and then they began brainstorming how their stories might weave together to create a piece.
> The next step in the process was to create a skill inventory, where each student would list on paper what skills they already had, everything from making signs, to writing poetry, speaking in public, making puppets, and organizing files. With this list, the students could imagine a form that their collaborative piece could take.[3]

She believes that everyone comes to her arts classes with a rich history to draw meaning from, and a set of unique talents to communicate that meaning. Past experiences are a framework with which to make sense of new ideas. And everyone walking in the door has something to offer the group from the very first day.

Understanding that no one is actually starting from zero helps in another way—it gives students a chance to feel a little more confident as they begin to sort out the social environment. For this particular class, which was to find its understanding of learning upended by the UnHappy Meal project, it would be useful to let the students feel they were standing on some familiar ground.

The very first week was to be critical, therefore, to give the students some room to create their own skills inventories, but also to establish the culture of this particular class. The new skills that they would need to learn and practice needed to be articulated from the beginning so that there was no confusion about what mattered.

The very first task for these ninth graders took no more than a week, and functioned as both an icebreaker and a method to introduce them to their new toolbox: presentation skills and the value of multiple drafts, and help them practice giving and receiving feedback, creating rubrics, and performing self-evaluation and reflection.

Most important, it would start them thinking about what learning and teaching actually are.

Mr. Werberger's Teacher Journal

I had a few sleepless nights thinking about this, but I was eventually nudged in the direction of having the kids practice teaching a short lesson to each other. Rather than having them do research on something scholarly, I decided that the students would each present a two minute lesson on a topic on which they considered themselves an expert. This would not be impromptu, exactly, as they had a night to prepare, but was meant only to be a quick, live demonstration to a small group of peers.

Something fun and casual, in other words, something that I could present as an icebreaker, nothing more.

The surprise for them is that this offhand, live lesson would eventually become a full-fledged, professional YouTube "How-To" video, but only after several other exercises that would teach them a few of the procedures they could expect to see with every project in the coming year.

Every student had to teach, and they taught in rounds. They were divided into three groups and expected to teach the same lesson multiple times, each time to a new audience.

For instance, each member of group A had to stand in a different part of the room, and teach to members of groups B and C for two minutes. Then the presenter would receive a new batch of Bs and Cs, and so on until every B and C had heard every member of A teach. At that point, it was the Bs turn to teach the As and Cs, and then the Cs taught. Each presenter thus taught the same lesson three or four times.

I watched kids instruct each other how to minimize anxiety by using pressure points, making chain mail bracelets, dancing, how to make a bed properly, and even the most efficient way to accidentally break one's iPhone. I had sympathy for the latter student, who told me she didn't feel particularly good enough at anything else to present on, but she did, in fact, manage to break her phone right before school started.

When it was over, I asked them how it felt to teach the very first time, and what changed for them as they redelivered the lesson. We also discussed what made an effective presentation—from enunciation and cadence to being able to convey enthusiasm and love for the subject.

Some discussion led to three rules that the students believed were the characteristics of a great presentation:

1. People should want to view it.
2. They should be able to understand it and then use it.
3. The whole thing should look professional (it should be clear that someone took care and effort into creating the presentation).

That all seemed appropriate enough—then the bomb dropped. Their real challenge was to turn that live lesson into a proper video tutorial for the whole world to see. Next, they should write down what they felt they had learned from the experience and what they would keep in mind as they worked on their video versions.

Student Journal: Maria

In my opinion, this exercise was one of the coolest things I've ever experienced. I am well aware that I probably chose one of the dumbest things to teach a lesson on, but still, it was fun. But you still had learned to understand how many components there are to being a teacher. While I was teaching, my brain had one thing going through it: How are you going to approach this?

And my mind, being the rattling can it is only said this back: I dunno, just teach them good.

Teach them good? How do I do that?

So I started by taking my favorite characteristic of teachers and applying it to myself. Energy. As I taught the two other people in front of me, I wanted them to keep their eyes on me. I found that as I was learning from others, I could get bored and distracted because they spoke quietly and/or monotonously. I made sure to keep a little bit of (awful) humor mixed in with my lesson, and spoke it all with a loud, clear, and excited voice.

Student Journal: Cady

As I developed my presentation I decided the most important thing about my lesson would be that I was comfortable teaching it. I made sure it was something I knew well (yoga) and that I could be pleased with the result, which I was hoping wouldn't end in disaster.

To be completely honest, I thought it went pretty well . . . mostly. Sure, it was frustrating when I was trying to discuss breathing techniques and people were rolling on the floor trying to show off all the poses they're experts in or falling into tables and chairs laughing hysterically. This also told me that, as I repeated the lesson to different groups, no one wanted to hear about breathing exercises or balance. People just wanted to see if they, too, could do downward dog or tree pose.

Finally, I cut the breathing and balance spiel down to ten seconds and skipped straight into yoga which definitely was better for holding people's attention. . . . Next time I will try to skip straight to the interesting parts to grab people's attention from the start.

Student Journal: Isaiah

Personally, I was quite nervous about teaching a subject without a rubric for two main reasons. First off, I was concerned about others judging me. I have only known my peers for about a week now, and am not sure the type of people they are. I found that after the first time teaching I was so nervous I rushed and stuttered, but only got positive feedback. Second, I was worried of not being able to fill the two minutes in which we had to teach. I knew if I didn't there would be an awkward silence, but if I spoke too slow people would lose interest. By the third attempt of teaching I felt confident and was able to speak more clearly.

If I had to add anything I think I would have wanted to create a more open atmosphere with a solid point and visual demonstration. In order to create a more conversational situation I would ask more questions. I found that if you read through a whole lecture people won't remember what their question was, I barely remember if I had lunch. To create a more visual demonstration I would actually draw. My drawing which I showed didn't explain my point if the multiple aspects to drawing . Last, I would ask people to draw something, because they're visual, auditory, and kinesthetic learners.

LEARNING ABHORS A VACUUM

The second consideration is that no one makes art alone. The students were going to have to get used to the idea that learning would come from interacting with each other, not just with the teacher. This did not mean all projects would be done in groups, but it did mean that all work would begin and end with conversations.

Artists build on the work of other artists. Artists may model their work on the work of their mentors, or they may deconstruct their mentor's work and rerepresent it. Older styles are rediscovered and reworked as a way to comment on work of the present. Idioms from one culture are adapted into another and remixed to present new fusions.

This is why the concept of copyright and infringement is such an important issue in the art world, and why so many artists make art that consciously rebels against this idea of ownership. In 1979, Sherrie Levine took pictures of Walker Evans's famous depression-era photographs and had them mounted in the Met in New York as her own work. Since then, Michael Mandiberg has taken pictures of Levine's copies and digitized them on his website, labeling those as *his* own work.

Everything that already exists is part of the materials by which new art is made. Artists place themselves into existing discourses and strive to make something new within it. Levine and Mandiberg's work are logical extremes of this approach, but are in a line with the notion that what has been created belongs to everyone.

Similarly, no one learns in a vacuum. The theory of social constructivism that runs through much progressive education in the twentieth century maintains that children actively make meaning of the world by interacting with others. In other words, the child is not an empty pitcher into which knowledge is poured. Rather, children gain understanding by filtering other people's experiences through their own perspective. Out of that comes learning. Constructivist education therefore builds upon the twin pillars of direct experience and social interactions.

One of the basic skills of the "21st Century Curriculum" (as created by the Partnership for 21st Century Learning [P21]) is working collaboratively. As mentioned before, this is hardly a new skill, and it was certainly a key component of John Dewey's educational philosophy.

The business world has also come to praise the virtues of collaboration. Corporate guru Scott Page argues in *The Difference* that a divergent group representing a multiplicity of perspectives and competencies is a critical asset for creative and efficient problem solving, and argues that companies should hire for "cognitive diversity." P21 was in fact created in partnership with business leaders, many of whom come from companies seeking international markets for both labor and products.

Yet collaboration is a tendentious part of the curriculum, having come to mean in many classrooms that students work jointly on a single project and conspire jointly on every decision. One aspect of the backlash against forced collaboration is that some students, rightly, prefer to work alone, while others point out that collaboration is rarely equal within groups, with some students dominating the work and others abstaining from doing their share.

Susan Cain, among others, has argued in *Quiet: The Power of Introverts in a World That Can't Stop Talking* that quiet introspection and working alone is at least as valuable as forced sharing. She also believes that creativity requires solitude, and that the bustle and roar of a collaborative session destroys the capacity for innovation.

Moreover, an experiment carried out at Berkeley's Haas School of Business found that when teams of four students worked together to solve math problems, the team leaders were not necessarily the best mathematicians—just the loudest. As Christopher Chabris and Daniel Simmons explain in *The Invisible Gorilla*, "For 94% of the problems, the groups' final answer was the first answer anyone suggested, and people with dominant personalities just tend to speak first and most forcefully."[4]

There is no guarantee that collective wisdom will discover the right solution—it often bends to the will of a leader who may have his own agenda, and who isn't introspective enough to suspect he may be wrong.

Finally, giving group grades for joint work is an easy way to come under fire for being unfair, while piecing out who did what in order to assign individual grades on group work is just as subjective and is even more arduous without a great deal of foreplanning. Sometimes teachers participate in the unforgivable sin that we make for all the right reasons—putting a high performer with a lower performing group in hopes that the go-getter will teach the others how to excel. Inevitably, the overachiever does all the work and resents the teacher for it.

One answer to this conundrum is that collaboration does not have to mean that each member of the class has to work in lockstep with each other on a single outcome. It is, rather, a function of seeing the other members of the group as a resource that can help one's own *individual* work.

Imagine the difference between a project in which every group member is working on the same task, and one in which each member of the group is doing what she feels she is strongest at, and most intrigued by—and consequently, solely creating her own piece of the puzzle.

To return to Naidus's earlier point, she had her students talk to each other to find the commonalities between their stories, and in the brainstorming stage, each listed their strengths—not to work together on those strengths, but because those abilities might be unique. Among my own students, casual conversations have revealed that some of them have already hunted and learned to dress game, while others have farming experience to be tapped (even if they don't know yet what's coming).

Thus, collaboration becomes a way for students to share their individual perspectives and talents and so enhance the potential for everyone to be successful on their own artifacts, rather than simply working on the same artifact together. The goal is to get students to learn to look at each other's work and offer each other the benefit of those multiple perspectives and talents.

In the first step of the Teaching Project, the students had been instructed to develop a lesson based on their own mastery, and then to teach their peers this skill. The second step would be to use each other's insights to make these lessons better.

Mr. Werberger's Teacher Journal

> We had watched a few how-to videos on the Internet already—everything from card tricks to cooking, and that, combined with their reflections, helped us to create a rubric to guide their video productions. The students' rubric was similar to the prior one they'd developed. Each video should:
>
> - Appeal aesthetically to the viewer.
> - Be clear enough to be used by a viewer immediately after viewing.
> - Be accurate in terms of its information.
> - Look as though genuine effort went into making it.
>
> I tasked the students with creating a rough draft of this video lesson, using the rubric to guide them. They posted this video to their blogs—as not yet worthy of general consumption. The videos were of varying quality overall, but I was surprised about the variety of approaches that emerged.
>
> Some students merely set up the laptop camera and spoke into it, while others had a friend film them while they carried out their demonstrations. A more enterprising student—the chain mail enthusiast—created a stop motion effect by linking images of each step of the process together into an animated short. Some students did everything they could to avoid being actually seen.
>
> That left me with the task of teaching them the next day how to give each other effective feedback (which would ultimately end up becoming the most ubiquitous form of collaboration over the year). To begin the conversation, we talked about times when they had received feedback that actually allowed them to improve—sometimes immediately. Naturally, few of those moments had occurred in school. Organized sports and music classes predominated discussion.

So, why does critique seem effective everywhere *but* in school, where it can be argued students receive feedback almost continually? Once they had listened to each other's stories, it became clear that *one* piece of critique, focused on *one* particular problem, and delivered physically and demonstrably—that is, with the hand moved into the correct position, or the jump shot readjusted—was the key to success. Not necessarily even kindness mattered so much as the impression the students got that getting that hand motion or shot release correct *really mattered*.

The rules were clear to everyone: if critique is not "just in time," it will go unused, and if it is not illustrated with the corrective, it won't be understood. The students were then moved immediately into feedback circles to review their first video drafts using the rubric. These rules (which were similar to those laid down by Ron Berger in his own work on critique) were:

- Be mindful of being supportive.
- Be constructive where possible.
- Be specific where possible.

This common understanding is critical, for it is the only way to build a sense of trust in a class of kids who are naturally insecure (they are thirteen, after all) and who are all new to each other. Without a sense of mutualism, students will give useless or even cruel feedback, and it will become harder and harder for students to show their own work to others. Modeling the correct form of feedback is critical at this stage, and it proved to be worthwhile to use previous student's work to practice on before moving on the real stuff.

The students browsed through each other's videos and offered critique on paper comment forms. It worked well enough as an exercise for the critics, but not so much as a way of generating useful guiding advice, as most students selected the same three videos to comment on. The problem was resolved later in the next go-round by having students write their comments in an electronic forum, making sure to choose drafts that had not yet been selected. Yet for this they had viewed a few examples and were presumably able to think about how their video rated in comparison to these others.

DEMONSTRATING WHAT YOU KNOW

There is some debate in the art world as to whether art must have an audience for it to indeed be "art." Some students believe creation can be a private act—as long as the artists tell themselves they have created art, then "art" it is. On the other hand, if one believes that art is a form of communication, then there must be a receiver of that message. Regardless of the finer points of the debate, artists must show a portfolio of work to gain public acknowledgment of their status as artists.

Similarly, teachers don't take the student's word for it that they are educated. Everyone has to show evidence that they have learned something before they are allowed to move on to the next task, unit, or grade level. The only argument is to the form of this demonstration, its purpose, and the size of the audience.

The standard method of presenting knowledge in so many schools is some sort of formal written assessment, an analysis of prelearned content knowledge, to be viewed by the teacher only. These tend to end up in the trash can eventually. Nor does much of this earlier work ever find its way into later essays and research papers. "Learning defenses" and portfolios that require students to comment on a year's worth of work to justify their graduation have mitigated this problem somewhat. How much farther can this kind of assessment be pushed?

Consider a work of art presented in an upper-level arts course. The piece is presented to the fellow members of the class. A formal critique is held. The artist is able to judge the effectiveness of the piece from the critique received; that is, was my message understood? The piece may be reworked until the message, the intent, is clearer, or the piece itself more unique within the discourse the artist is working.

The art piece will at some point be presented to a larger audience. Different stages of that artifact's creation, or even of the artists' entire opus, may accompany it. Sometimes, there is no final piece, only a series of experiments. Thus, everything—the title, the physical site of the exhibit, the other pieces around which the work is shown—contributes to the meaning of the piece that the audience will construct for itself. This is the theory of reception, that an artist and the audience are in a dialogue together and collectively shape that artwork.

So, what happens if one melds reception theory into educational design theory? That is, what if one holds student artifacts from a history or science class up to the same standards as art, and judges the effectiveness of student work partly on the response from the public? Could a history project have a social context based on where it is viewed, and for whom it has been created? Does that create different pressures and stresses than delivering an assignment for a teacher's eyes only? More important, does that create different motivations?

This, then, was the reason for creating a rough draft of a teaching video and conducting rounds of peer review. The final challenge for the students came next: turning that two-minute draft into a professional presentation for a larger audience, which meant posting their polished videos to YouTube.

The point was not simply to use technology, of course. Technology in this case existed only to capture their voice and their actions for repeated viewing in a public space. The real purpose was to get them used to being experts and sharing their expertise.

Animals are capable of using tools, though they may not be as technologically advanced. Thus, we should want students not just to use tools, but to think about how they use them to show their abilities—to be able to articulate that. Cooking an egg required a certain facility in the kitchen, as did the use of a GoPro to capture the process. Thinking about the keys to a successful presentation was another tool, as was the ability to give useful feedback to help another student improve.

We should repeatedly ask students to share their knowledge with an audience, and they have a full range of means to do so—from drawing a picture to making a speech to making an object by hand. Whatever means of communication they choose, we want it to be because they consciously understand the potential of that form and what it is capable of accomplishing—not just because they've just always done it that way. Just as artists choose their media to communicate a message, so should they.

This was also the purpose for the students to keep a blog. Blogging carries with it the implicit assumption that one's writing is meant to be read—regardless of how hidden it is, it exists in public space. Yes, blog templates are fun to personalize, and yes, it is fun to add jpegs and movies to punctuate one's writing. But it is first and foremost a space for sharing ideas and receiving feedback apart from the usual suspects a student engages with. This last point relates to the final set of tools the students needed to practice with—self-reflection, or the ability to discern what had actually been learned.

GAUGING HOW FAR YOU'VE COME

If art is a method of understanding one's place in relation to the object of study, artists therefore need to be able to see themselves not as just that object. For a student, that would mean recognizing where they had started before the project began, and how much they had learned from the experience. Were they different now, somehow? Could they articulate what they had changed from the original artifact they'd created, and why?

Mr. Werberger's Teacher Journal

> I surprised them when I said that the reedited version of their video was not the actual assessment. I asked them instead to evaluate themselves—to consider how successful they had been at driving viewer interest, providing useful examples and commentary, putting forth their best effort, and so on. I also wanted to know how aware they were, here in this first week, of what they did and did not know
>
> I also asked them to give me their general thoughts on the project—generally, this was some version of "what did you learn, what's working so far, and what should we change or do next?"

Student Journal: Johann

> I'm really getting to learn how bad we are at doing some very important things. I really enjoy talking about how we could philosophically

improve a broken system, and when we started talking about Peer Editing, I secretly got very excited because it will act as a catalyst for so many more discussions on how we could improve society and our ways of life.

I took away from this how to really take and give feedback in an important way. Feedback changes the way we make something literally better, and as such a crucial point it's important we understand how to do it correctly. I've also started to learned how to manage my time better, which is an invaluable skill that will keep with me throughout my whole life.

I like how open you are with deadlines but don't constantly run around telling us that we're behind or need to get on it, because you know that we know. I also really like how in class that we have a lot of open space for points and counterpoints, discussions and debates, as I feel it adds a lot of perspective and intuition by seeing both sides of an argument thoroughly.

Student Journal: Tilly

Well, I watched my video many times before I could even start to give myself feedback. I'm very hard on myself. I had to remember not to be too hard but not go super easy. So I put a lot of planning into my video. I thought about all the different ways people learned and tried to incorporate that into my video. I wrote script after script to try and see what was informative and was entertaining at the same time. I also tried very hard to speak clearly and not talk super fast. But there was one thing in the video that bothered me a lot—my background wasn't the best choice. I went through all that planning and made a bad decision. I also wished I had done something a little more tech-savvy but that's not really my strong suit so I stuck to the basics for that part of it. Overall, I was happy with my video. I worked hard.

I was trying to think of some things I have learned. And I really learned how to use the Internet and YouTube and it really got a different part of my brain working. I now know a lot more about that kind of stuff.

Student Journal: Neil

What am I learning so far in class? Well, I've learned how to use technology in a more active manner, and that is very helpful, considering that we are surrounded by it. I've learned (sort of) how to teach and present things, which is a very helpful thing! But, to be honest, I haven't learned much. However, in the past weeks I have found that I am getting curious. Curious about the world, about how to make rice, about the Zapatista rebellion in Mexico; curious about anything, really. I hope that that leads somewhere; curiosity is a terrible thing to waste.

What's working well for me? I do like the straightforward approach utilized by our teacher and my fellow comrades-in-books. I also like the increased role technology has in class—it is really quite a liberating feeling. We have class discussions on things, which I like—communication is good in any relationship between people, be it in school or otherwise. If people are communicating, it leaves little room for confusion. Also, the assignments always seem to be pretty creative, which lets me really get into depth with them. I hope this is of use!

What isn't working well? I don't have any gnawing fears and hatred for history at the moment; it's going pretty well. I do hope that we don't get too technological—don't get me wrong, I do love laptops and Tumblr, but the humble paper and pen are versatile tools. They're uncomplicated. No walk-through is needed to write a paper.

Anything to add? Not really. I would like lots more stuff to do in class, just to keep the proverbial juices flowing. It also preps me for homework; gets me in the proper mindset for World Civ. Other than that, I got nothing.

NOTES

1. Beverly Naidus, *Arts for Change: Teaching Outside the Frame* (Oakland: New Village Press, 2009), 9.

2. Michael Michalko, "Twelve Things You Were Not Taught in School about Creative Thinking," Creativity Post, December 6, 2011, http://www.creativitypost.com/create/twelve_things_you_were_not_taught_in_school_about_creative_thinking.

3. Naidus, *Arts for Change*, 49.

4. Christopher Chabris and Daniel Simmons, *The Invisible Gorilla: And Other Ways Our Intuition Deceives Us*, Kindle ed. (New York: Harmony, 2010), 98.

THREE

Building a Culture of Learning and Exploration

Once an artist knows the medium, and knows the tools, they must be inspired to use them. As Neil said in his reflection, "curiosity is a terrible thing to waste." Curiosity is a tool like any other, but it is also a kind of paradox. It leads to a process of inquiry based on that desire to know, but the truly curious can never be satisfied. There will always be another question based on what was uncovered during the search for answers.

To give them a chance to play with this notion, the students will be asked to solve a problem using their curiosity rather than by drawing upon their knowledge. The path will be visible, but they have to learn to see it. By the end, they will be asked to turn around and see if they can figure out how they got there.

INFINITE QUESTIONS

Artists begin with a question in mind. They may not be able to articulate it, sometimes not until the piece is finished, but they sense there's a problem with the way things are. Something leaps out because it appears special or doesn't seem to fit with the rest.

Artists feel a pull to investigate this oddity. It might result in a new perspective on a familiar topic—that is, "Is there something else a chair can be?" It might result in a critique of an existing practice. It might result in the creation of a new technique, or a different use for a tool that already exists. The work they make dares the audience to question what they thought they knew to be true.

For this project to have the same effect, the students are going to need to learn how to see like a child again. They will need to learn how to trust their instincts, that whatever strikes them as odd is worth investigating. It will be so compelling they will want to learn more about it. The questions that come up for them have to be the ones that speak to their soul—the first ones that arise in their minds, not the ones a teacher plants for them to find.

The challenge is that the Happy Meal is so commonplace they have learned essentially not to notice it. They will look at a packet of ketchup, and to the extent they think about it at all, it will be to say, "yeah, so that's ketchup, so what?" We want them to wonder how they got that stuff in the little plastic bag, or who was the first person to figure out it went with fries, or who the person was who packed it in there and what they were thinking that particular day.

If they are going to reconstruct this meal in a creative way, every item in there must be open to question. They will need to take this meal apart, piece by piece, and really study what's in there. This should be as free as possible, allowing for surprise, for accidental discovery, for an abrupt loss of interest, to being able to leave an idea alone for a while and come back to it when ready. We, as teachers, just need to stay out of the way as much as we can.

In eight months, there will be a path of learning that is discernible upon looking back, but it won't feel like it while the students are on it. There will be discontinuities, dead ends, errors that will trip them up. They will feel lost before they are found. As a teacher, we will have to fight the urge to direct, to take control. They will have to find their way out of the woods themselves. The most we will be able to do is hand them a lamp.

> When we refuse . . . we create dissonance and more important, we allow dissonance to continue—when we enter a classroom and we refuse to call it to order, we are allowing study to continue, dissonant study perhaps, disorganized study, but study that precedes our call and will continue after we have left the room.[1]

Here is the notion of critical exploration. Students must learn to take intellectual risks and learn to see and think differently. They need to learn how to ask questions and investigate how to answer them.

This is inquiry-based education, nothing new, but we want to add a twist: We want to make this process an infinite loop—or at least, a long eight-month process of constant renegotiation. We actually don't want answers. As soon as students think they have solved a problem, we want them to keep developing questions about it. They shouldn't ever feel they have closed the case—only that there's still more to discover.

LEARNING TO TAKE RISKS

Creation is an act of critique. It begins with a perception of the world as it is and then challenges it. The creator is daring to see things differently than what is accepted as true. What is then made is unique. But it has to begin with the willingness to disagree that whatever is, is all there must be.

Often, American classrooms invert the world's assumptions about our own intellectual values. People overseas tend to see Americans as brash, unorthodox thinkers, constantly tinkering with rules and systems, burning down the past in order to build the future. We have successfully exported the notion of ourselves as heroic pragmatists—like Edison and his thousands of patents, or Jobs and his belief in simple design.

The US tradition of economic growth was built on the idea that there's always a better way to make a product—the result is that the standard American history textbook tends to explain our industrial growth as a mixture of unlimited resource and innovative spirit. The truth of the matter may be more nuanced, but myths have their power, and regardless of what Carnegie, Rockefeller, and Vanderbilt did to crush innovations that threatened them, they did owe their rise to their revolutionary ideas about design, manufacturing, and organization.

So, why do American classrooms seem to create the opposite effect in students—a culture of providing safe answers to rote questions and avoiding critical engagement. Some of that herd mentality is no doubt from social pressures to avoid standing out, but some educators also believe the fault lies in the educational culture in many of our middle and high schools.

The pressure to perform well on tests is part of the problem, and so is the emphasis on control. Problems are simple to solve if you memorize the formula or the content, and a "keep their butts in the seats" philosophy of pedagogy does not create an environment for innovation.

Modern educators are becoming more and more aware of the research into neuroscience that tells us how our brains work most effectively, and we understand that children may be kinetic, auditory, or visual learners, that some may talk more while others think better by walking around, but we still ask students to demonstrate learning by the traditional means of tests, essays, quizzes, and demonstrations. So much learning technology is just transferring an oral presentation into a PowerPoint, and a PowerPoint into a movie—same thing in a different form.

University of Oregon College of Education professor Yong Zhao, author of *World Class Learners: Educating Creative and Entrepreneurial Students*, advocates that students become entrepreneurs and seek opportunities to use school projects to make objects that other people might buy, rather than doing more traditional kinds of school work.

When asked whether there was a place for essay writing in his ideal curriculum, he answered that anything his daughter might do in school that didn't offer the opportunity for earning income was kind of a waste of time.

That wasn't a glib response—he meant it. His vision of the future is a school system that builds on what he believed America has always done best—to promote a paradigm of education he terms "entrepreneur oriented," as apart from the "employee-oriented."

In his words:

> The employee-oriented paradigm aims to transmit a prescribed set of content (the curriculum and standards) deemed to be useful for future life by external authorities, while the entrepreneur-oriented aims to cultivate individual talents and enhance individual strengths. The employee-oriented paradigm produces homogenous, compliant, and standardized workers for mass employment while the entrepreneurial-oriented education encourages individuality, diversity, and creativity.

The good news is that while our students may not test well compared to students in other countries, especially in math, we seem to lead the world in confidence. Zhao believes that confidence is as important as content knowledge, especially when it comes to challenging traditions and innovating.[2]

As positive as that sounds, is there yet room for improvement? Can we create an even more innovative and creative student body? Can we radically reevaluate the role of the teacher in the classroom, the nature of what is testable, the manner in which content is learned to stress divergent thinking and creativity first? How would that be different from what we have now? The first step may not even to be to throw out the textbooks, though that's easily enough done. Rather, it may be to teach our subjects as crafts, rather than disciplines.

Arts classes, unlike most other school subjects, require students not just to learn form and technique, but to *make* what they study. Students make art. They "craft." Students in history classes don't *make* history. Generally, they study what other people have already said about the past and they write about it. Occasionally, a student develops a rudimentary theory on his or her own, but they aren't required to do so in order to pass the class, and they certainly don't go off and write a book about it to prove it.

So, what does a classroom prepared for divergent thinking look like?

A colleague, Dennis, tells a story of how he begins his arts class each year. He asks the students to collaborate on a wall mural on the very first day. He rearranges the room so that all the desks are pushed into corners, and everyone is seated, facing each other, around a roughly ten foot by ten foot square of layered newspaper. He gives them the media they asked for, and then simply says to them: "Draw something!"

Dennis recounts:

> Invariably, they end up creating their own space. Some students are more bold and brazen than others, and try something big—usually their own name—and everyone looks shocked. They look to me to see what my reaction is, but I try to have an emotionless mask. Once they have created their own contained drawing, their own borders, I have them stand up and move three or four paces to the right, and start to draw again.
>
> Some people will be very polite and just kind of color in what's already there, or work around it. Others are like, "I don't give a crap," and just go over it. I just let it happen, switching media back and forth for however long it takes.
>
> What generally happens is—the important part—that students just realize nothing is going to work, that it's pointless. They start "cliquing" together . . . and no one is paying attention to each other. It agitates them, pisses them off, because they are forced to work on the same thing together but they aren't working together. It raises tension in the room. Sometimes students recognize this immediately and take charge of running a group conversation to create something in common.
>
> This year, I had a big class, and after four classes one of the girls finally snaps and takes it out on me, saying, "This is b.s.! You're making us work on this thing and it's not going to happen. No one's listening to anyone." I stopped class, and made everyone put their things down.
>
> This was my window. A student had finally broken down and it gave me a chance to talk about the fear that makes us gravitate to people who are familiar to us, to use the materials we are comfortable with, and it keeps us separated. "All we will get out of this is a pile of crap if you aren't willing to get past your fear of talking to people who are different from you, or trying new experiences. Get out of the bubble and make it work!"
>
> It was a heavy moment, but the girl who had started this went right to the board and started asking people what they wanted to create. It was beautiful. The final piece didn't work conceptually, or compositionally, but they were able to work through it and make art that did eventually work.
>
> That lesson is always a risk. I might know what I'm going to do, but I always throw in a variable—I always want the potential to fail. If I exercise that, it allows the students to do that, too. It's good to show them when you fail, and admit to it, and get up and continue.

What would happen if the teacher sat a student down in a history class, on the very first day, and said, "do some history"? What responses would they get? Would that command even be understood? More to the point, why haven't the students been asked that?

In that respect, we teachers are just as crippled by fear as Dennis's students. The idea of a project failing is terrifying, as is the potential for our own ignorance or ineffectiveness to be revealed to our students. Students have told stories of teachers who made up facts—easily verifiable online—rather than admit they don't know the answer to a question.

What can a history teacher do to break the model of structured projects, of "right answers" and "correct skills sets," of formal research papers or PowerPoint presentations of a depressing sameness?

Let's revisit an earlier quote from Bevery Naidus that described part of the process of creation in an adult arts class:

> [W]e would invite students to meet in small groups to share a social issue that affected them personally, on a gut level. . . . One student was worried about the growing global disappearance of clean water. She didn't feel she was truly confronting that issue emotionally on a daily basis, but working on the topic was a good way to avoid dealing with more immediate problems. . . . We talked about a way that she could combine her more intellectual but still very valid concern, with the emotional ones that ruled her daily stress. . . . *One way to describe this process is to say that it means working from the core, rather than from what you think you should be talking about in your art.*[3]

What Naidus says here is that student creativity begins with the personal, not the political—the issues that students confront in their daily lives that elude simple classification into "history," "science," or "literature." What if a history teacher could connect the emotional turbulence of a teenager's inner world to those grander issues that continually roil the outer world—why wars happen, what is justice or fairness, what is the social effect of new technologies, how do we manage our resources most effectively?

If we can make the subject of a typical history investigation intensely personal and individual to them, students will be less worried about finding the "right" answer. They might feel freer to experiment, less inclined to fall into traditional patterns of obedience to authority's desires. Are we able to create Elliot Eisner's "pursuit of surprise"?

Again, if the goal of an engineer is to build a product that meets the goal, artists seem to spend the majority of their time just trying to understand what the goal is. That's what should happen in class.

Therefore, the first challenge is to get the students to see with their own eyes, and to ask questions that come from their hearts.

LEARNING TO SEE, LEARNING TO THINK, LEARNING TO ASK

The thinking exercise called "See, Think, Wonder," appears to have originated from the Harvard Graduate School of Education as part of a project called Visible Thinking. The goal, as the name suggests, is to make the cognitive process apparent for students, rather than leave a mystery. It also lets the teacher know what they find interesting or inexplicable, so it makes their thinking not just visible to each other but to teachers as well.

The routine helps students develop a critical eye and learn to ask investigative questions—much like a detective. In fact, one can turn any history lesson into an exercise in criminal forensics by showing an artifact—a photograph, a document, a piece of art—and asking students to perform three simple exercises in order to "solve the crime," or what they think the importance of the image is:

- To See—to note the details that stand out or seem important
- To Think—to ponder what these details might mean
- To Wonder—to ask questions based on these details or your hypotheses from step two

The upcoming project, the UnHappy Meal, offered a natural topic for the students to investigate—our relationship to food. This thinking routine led naturally into inquiry and investigation, and the subsequent writing process would include peer-critique and self-evaluation. Finally, thanks to the subsequent blogging platform that was chosen to present student work, their writing would be undertaken with a wider audience ultimately in mind.

Mr. Werberger's Teacher Journal

In this case, I used images from the book *Hungry Planet* by Peter Menzel and Faith D'Aluisio, which portrayed pictures of families from around the world, each with a week's worth of food spread out before them. I started the kids off with a portrait of a "typical" middle-class American family and their pantry, with instructions to note every detail they saw in the picture (without worrying about its importance). I then asked them to develop hypotheses about this family from these details.

The students then compared and contrasted this picture with those of families from Latin American, African, and Asian countries. They noticed the difference in the quantities and types of fresh foods versus processed foods, and vegetables versus starches, among other things, and were instructed again to develop hypotheses about what these similarities and differences might mean.

Finally, I asked them to think of questions they needed answered to prove their hypotheses. At first, the students operated at a basic level—looking for statistics on the typical American diet in terms of food type and calories, for instance, or their costs. As these first, generic questions were answered in their investigations, I pushed them to start asking deeper and more creative questions. Some wondered whether the amount of food was any indication of family's quality of life, and others were even more philosophical, asking whether Americans were in fact "happy," and if not, who in fact was.

Student Journals: Jacob and Cady

Looking at the average American family's weekly food intake, it seems like they are very busy. Bananas, granola bars, frozen food, fast food, chips, and greasy snacks are all things that are easy to eat in a hurry. Why? Why is the average American family so busy?

Is the average American family paranoid about not having enough food? If you look at the American family compared to the family from Kuwait, there is a lot more food [for American families]. Even if you compare the American family with the family from Beijing, the Americans still have more. Are Americans paranoid that they won't have enough food?

Student Journals: Jessi and Natalya

In the first picture [Ecuador] the family has a lot of vegetables and you hardly see wheat products and they have to feed a family of nine people. We also noticed that the house that the photo was taken in is very dark and it appears that they are sitting in hay and are living in a handmade brick home. In the second picture [Mali,] there are fifteen people living in one household. In this picture they have mainly grains and some vegetables. We think that they have to control how much they eat in a week because they don't have enough resources to eat all they want like other parts in the world. This shows that people with less money find ways to survive through obstacles.

Questions:

- How much junk food do Americans eat?
- How much do supermarkets profit out of junk food?
- In other countries, how much do they spend on food that they don't grow?
- How much do Americans spend on food that they don't grow?

LEARNING TO INVESTIGATE

The point of doing this as a research assignment was not merely to ask questions, of course, but to engage with them—to answer them if possible, or if not, to refine them further. Therefore, ask students to develop "research declarations"—or statements of intent, that required them to explain why they had become interested in examining certain abstract questions, and to break these questions into smaller wonderings that could more easily be researched.

Spend one or two days challenging students to find resources related to these questions, and having them justify why they felt these sources passed the smell test—that is, whether the information they found was sourced correctly, or whether the authors were certified to give them this information and hence, were trustworthy. Their peers can double check these sources and give them a second opinion.

While the teacher felt this was "working"—in the sense that the students seemed industrious and happily surfing on their own—the real question was where to go next with this stuff. A research paper seemed so uninteresting to write—and to read—after all this work. What could the students create that might achieve a wider readership, or have some sort of impact on the issues they were happily investigating?

Mr. Werberger's Teacher Journal

> I had a moment of insight while reading about the way young activists were using blogs and other social media to carry out on-the-spot reporting and to bypass the big news agencies. As I saw it, the students had asked questions on the topics they were interested in—why not ask them to be reporters? Moreover, they had identified "good" websites by focusing on the way information was presented, cited, or otherwise verified; on the way the authors of the site presented themselves and their credentials; and furthermore, by whether the website had "viewer appeal" and offered opportunities to take action or learn more. Thus, I challenged them to write a blog that looked professional, trustworthy, and led to action. I called it the Social Activist Blog for lack of any real creativity. I told them that if they had gotten a wild hair to read about something they personally found compelling, they should feel they can use what they learn to make a difference in the world. We read blogs, determined what an effective post looked, and found we could use our original rubrics for the teaching videos—appeal, clarity (also called usefulness), content, and work ethic as the main categories. They spent about three class days writing and researching and continuing to critique each other's drafts. The students were getting a little better already at adopting a critical voice, and were sussing out issues I would have flagged myself.

EXAMPLES OF STUDENT CRITIQUES

Paul to Neil

> The opening paragraph is perfect. It gave a good idea that we might not know a lot, teased a bit of information, and also let us know what to expect. Then you went crazy with information. I feel like you kinda just threw numbers at us, making it hard for us to remember anything other than that a lot of babies, more than a small town in New York, die.

I like that you gave a way to support the problem that you faced, which showed you had genuine care for the topic. I think as a small improvement to the eyes, and to make your blog a more readable amount (ironic because mine was so much longer than yours, and yours was so quick and nice to read), you could've included the pictures directly into the text, rather than making them all the way at the top so you have to scroll down to get to the information. Or you could've included a little "blurb" of information with the pictures giving a tease as to what the post is about.

Isaiah to Paul

I really enjoyed reading your blog. It was a very interesting topic, while being abstract. The main issues I had were some of the formatting. The photo split the lines making it look a little unprofessional. Also when you said "We experience happiness through objects" doesn't that conflict with your morals that you can't buy happiness. If so, what is happiness? Is it true happiness or what pop culture has defined as happiness?

Think about it. Sure you become excited when you get something, but within a few minutes you have lost that feeling. True happiness should last a while in your heart. Shouldn't it? Also when you wrote "I am satisfied with my life" what does "satisfied" mean? Does it mean we can obtain our basic needs of water, food, health, education, and shelter or is it when we have obtained more than needed? Other than those few thoughts I really liked your blog.

BeBe to Isaiah

Isaiah is doing health problems of the countries by comparing them. The steps are very clear. It points out the reference numbers and websites, so we can see the details from the post. And the idea about diet is strong, . . . now people always think about dying, but not lack of health. I have few comments about his main ideas expression.

First, about the death rate, I think it is not all about health. It is also connected to the other problem, so it should not all line up with the health problem. Second, I think you can also put the health rate in it, for reference, so people can see more about it. Third, not all diets are bad, it depends on (self-)control, and working out.

The students used peer feedback, as well teacher input, to refine their blogs, if necessary. They were told that their work needed to reach competence before it could go out into the world—no "C" efforts passed muster, though they would have multiple opportunities to reedit their work to get it up to code.

AN INTERLUDE FOR FEEDBACK FEEDBACK

This format—the introduction of a thinking routine to stimulate observations and questions at the beginning of each new topic, the formulation of an inquiry-based investigation from those observations and questions, and the subsequent rounds of writing, critique, and rewriting—essentially became the working formula for the rest of the school year. Over time, the students' critiques grew better, their insights more perspective, and the detail they provided ever richer.

However, it proved harder to get the students to use that feedback in their writing. They were still waiting for the voice of the authority in the room—the teacher—to point out what needed fixing before they acted. There was also as yet no mechanism to assess the quality of the feedback the students were giving. The questions thus became, how does one convince the students to read and consider the feedback they receive, and how can the students who weren't pushing their critical abilities be persuaded to give more effort?

Mr. Werberger's Teacher Journal

> I decided that rather than just letting students provide feedback to each other, and then grading that critique myself, I would let the receivers of that feedback speak back to their critics. Let them grade each other based on how effective and helpful the critique is. Much of the feedback has been relentlessly positive in a nonhelpful way—lots of rahrahing, as though they are afraid of insulting each other. I wanted to give the students a chance to define the kind of feedback they want to receive.
>
> So this is "Feedback Feedback." It feels a bit like those moments in a panel discussion or in an op-ed when the presenter is able to respond to reviewers. A good skill! And it lets me know what the students themselves found helpful (and forces them to read the critique, let's not forget).

EXAMPLE 1

Yvette's Original Critique of Javier's Work

> For Appeal—I give you an excellence. You were very "down to earth."
> You explained everything well and best of all it was interesting
> For Content—I give you a standard. Sorry dude. I mean sure you covered almost everything but it was very broad and unfocused and you had everything there—you just had to make it more detailed. Also go

more into why corn is so bad and why processed corn is thirteen out of thirty-eight ingredients in a chicken nugget.

For Usefulness—I give you a standard for almost the same reason I gave you a standard on the last one but to add, you did not give links or pictures or how I can help stop this and feed my kids and friends healthier food. Plus, without super detailed info how am I supposed to know enough to help myself.

For Workmanship—I give you a "needs improvement" because your lack of effort really brought down the whole quality of your blog. I mean you have the potential but you just have to put in the effort.

Zack's Original Critique of Javier's Work

I liked how you got straight to the point in your blog post. If a blog post is too long I usually end up not reading it. Also, I like how you gave examples for your argument claiming how bad fast food is for you. I never knew that almost all the food is made out of corn.

Javier's Feedback Feedback to Critiquers Yvette and Zack

As far as Yvette's feedback goes, I found it to be very useful. She really did a good job pointing out what I did well, and what I need to improve on. After reading Yvette's feedback I realized that while I was on the right track, my writing was a little dull, and I talked too broadly. I am also I little disappointed because I put good effort into this post, yet it did not really shine through.

As with Zack's feedback, it just seemed really half-assed to me. I just felt like there was no real "feedback," nothing to work with. His feedback was very blunt, and I just felt like it was more of a forced compliment than a real piece of feedback. Overall, I thought Yvette gave some strong feedback, though it would have been nice for a little more elaboration. Zack on the other hand, did not give very useful feedback, for it was too broad, and while it was all compliments, there was nothing really specific.

EXAMPLE 2

Neil's Critique of Paul's Blog Post

'Twas very interesting—your post. I particularly enjoyed how you not only discussed how meat suppliers weren't so very "clean" in their handling of the meat, but you also described the apathy many consumers displayed while eating fast food which they knew was bad. That is probably even scarier than the part about the meat! You were very descriptive and clear, but your post wasn't too drawn out and lengthy. You had your sources present and you had just enough information. Not so much that you're drowning in it, but not so little that you're left guessing.

If I could change anything, I would just ask you to describe the negative health effects of eating this outdated meat. How is it bad? Is it much worse than not-so rotten beef? Can we directly prevent this old meat from getting into our food? If so, how?

Paul's Feedback to Neil

Great feedback. I loved the in-depth compliments which gave me an idea of what is pleasing to the eye. Also you gave very good negative feedback. I totally agree that it was lengthy, and to be honest I think it was total garbage. I was rushed. I was stressed by the due date. If I had had an extra week to do the project I think I would make many changes. Though how would you recommend decreasing the length? I personally think each topic made a different point, and each were necessary. Then again that is just my opinion.

Also, then in conflict with the previous statement you recommend me to explain more. . . . It's a great idea, but then it would be even more lengthy. I feel my point would be more effective in another complete blogpost do to the many different aspects about the health issues. All in all I think out of the three reviews I received yours was the best, even though there were some grammatical errors.

In many cases, the students wrote feedback that was more or less similar to that which they had received from the teacher—pointing out a lack of sources or citations, not adequately explaining terms or why the issue they were addressing was an actual problem, grammatical mistakes (which is at the shallow end of peer critique, but practice matters,) missing steps, or even logical inconsistencies in their arguments.

FINAL BLOG AND REFLECTION

The students were asked to choose the top three blogs, which would be posted on other forms of social media. Isaiah had been curious about the rate of disease and death between people in Japan and in the United States, and to what degree diet was a factor. BeBe, Frederick, and Thomas, who were all from China, collaborated on a long post in which they discussed the injustice that those who picked the food often couldn't afford to buy it.

Here is the third blog, as well as the student's postblog reflection. The student, Jason, had been interested in the lifestyle of the Kuwaiti family depicted in *Hungry Planet,* and without knowing anything about the country, was curious if the family existed at the higher or lower end of the country's wealth distribution.

From Jason: Is Kuwait in Need of Help?

Kuwait. It's somewhere in the Middle East, right? Probably impoverished. Probably in need of foreign aid. Is it, though?

We can start by looking at the Human Development Index, an annually published document created by the United Nations. It's a sort of quality of life measurement, with scores for Health, Education, Living Standards, and a grand total. Kuwait ranks, out of all surveyed countries, 67th in Health, 124th in Education, 6th in Living Standards, and 62nd total. As a reference point, the United States scores 38th in Health, 5th in Education, 10th in Living Standards, and 3rd total.

Another fact we can look at is gross national income per capita. This is usually referred to as "average income," which may or may not be accurate for a country like Kuwait where nearly half of the GDP comes from the oil industry. In fact, the Kuwait Petroleum Corporation and its subsidiaries are owned by the Kuwaiti government. The "average income" in Kuwait is pretty close to that of the United States, however, according to a blog on the *Kuwaiti Times*, prices are high for rent, food, and everyday items.

Now, let's try to get some insight from external sources about the living conditions of Kuwait. This is tricky. Official information is hard to find, and lots of statistics are simply missing from the UNICEF page — dashes show up where numbers should be. However, I was able to find a couple of somewhat less official sources: a site called InterNations and a *New York Times* article.

InterNations is a site with the goal of "make life easier for expatriates!" and the Living in Kuwait article I read talks about the "booming economy" and the "international schools for your kids." Of course, we shouldn't forget about the "extensive social welfare services, employment, and housing," and the "large, professional expat community." Funny thing: I have only seen pictures of white people on this website. It seems to have a pretty specific target audience.

The *New York Times* article is a little different. It tells of immigrant maids and their "unpaid wages," "lack of legal protection," "physical or sexual abuse," and even an employer that "threw [the maid] out of a third-floor window, breaking her back." This is quite a contrast to the InterNations article.

For such a small country, Kuwait is a complicated place. Some people get rich, some people run away, and most people are immigrants or expatriates. There's lots of oil, no taxes, and it's rarely talked about. I guess it's easy to forget about the little country next to Iraq with the white kids going to school and the maids huddling in embassies. Does it need help? It's got food and water, but it does need better laws and regulations.

Now who wants some oil money?

From Jason's Self-Assessment

Appeal: Standard. I think the writing is understandable and at least engaging enough that I can read through it. I've got a couple of screen-shots, which I guess count as pictures. I haven't done anything with the background of my blog, but it's not terrible (no Comic Sans!).

Content: Standard. Statistics all come from governmental or international organizations and all sources are directly linked in-text. Post stays on pretty much the same topic all the way through, and doesn't use offensive phrases, but isn't too formal and dry either.

Usefulness: Standard. Doesn't say much about what the reader can do for the situation, but has examples of different perspectives on Kuwait. I can't judge too accurately how well I explain things, since I already know what I mean, but I'd say it wasn't too hard to understand.

Workmanship: Standard. Uses a good font (always important!), wasn't done on a phone, and I looked over it many times before posting it (being insecure about my writing helped). Was turned in on time, although I accidentally spent almost all of my Algebra I class in the library working on it. (Oops!)

What have I learned over the past week, and what would I like to do next? I've had a bit of a reminder that the Middle East isn't just a blob of countries, where people fight and starve and not much else, but actually has some pretty complex things going on that don't have to do with war. Plus, I've had some more experience with writing in blog style, and figured out a pretty good system for writing and viewing materials more efficiently (write on the iPad, look at web pages on the library computer). Finally, I've had a valuable lesson about the importance of checking your schedule before going to study.

Next, I'd like to keep writing blog posts like the Kuwait one. It was interesting to dig for information and get around the lack of publicity.

This was a case in which the formal product was less important than the artifacts the students created to show their thinking. The point of the "big project," again, was not just to write a research paper or make a Happy Meal—it was to use the project as a kind of safety net to allow the students to pursue whatever stimulated their curiosity. Their writing was becoming a blend of introspection and external detail—a style that was placing them at the center of the topics they chose to investigate.

It was now October, and the unveiling of the UnHappy Meal could not be put off any longer.

NOTES

1. Stefano Harney and Fred Moten, *The Undercommons: Fugitive Planning and Black Study* (Minor Compositions, New York, 2013), 9.
2. Yang Zhao, "Numbers Can Lie: What TIMSS and PISA Truly Tell Us, if Anything?" December 11, 2012, http://zhaolearning.com/2012/12/11/numbers-can-lie-what-timss-and-pisa-truly-tell-us-if-anything/#_ftn33.
3. Naidus, *Arts for Change*, 49; emphasis added.

FOUR

Deconstruction

Some teachers excel at luring students into learning. Like master chefs, they set a table so appetizing that students can't help themselves but take a bite. Hunger might be the best sauce, but curiosity is close behind.

The students had been wondering why they were learning about food in what was supposed to be a world history class. Mostly, they were happy to do so if it meant avoiding textbooks, but as yet there seemed to be no higher purpose to it. But they wouldn't be content to continue their current explorations without some new trigger to keep their momentum going. They didn't know yet what they were being prepared for. They needed their curiosity to be renewed.

They were also about to begin a task common to both engineers and artists: dismantling an object to see how it works. Like engineers, they would be tasked to recreate the object that lay before them. To know it, they would have to take it apart. They would identify every component and a strategy for making it. They would have to understand each piece's characteristics—the amounts, the colors, the shapes, the textures—and how each related to the whole. That is one method of seeing.

Yet they would also become artists, in which this dissection would lead them to thinking more deeply about consumption, about health, about our social organization, and what each of them believes is the right way to live. This is the second way to see—to understand how much more an object could be than it appears.

It was time to set the table, in this case, quite literally, with the Happy Meal itself.

THE IMPORTANCE OF THE ENTRY EVENT

The entry event is the lure for the project. It separates an authentic, personal experience from the more typical project rollouts we all endured in school. Consider that nearly every year from sixth to twelfth grade students are assigned some sort of research paper in a typical history class, for which the introduction goes something like this:

A three to four page leaflet is passed around the room. This manifesto contains all the instructions and specifications for completing the project, things like to which corner the staple should be affixed, whether the students have to include page numbers, the type and size of the font. The topic is usually constrained to a broad timeframe or theme, with a list of sample questions the students can choose from if they can't think of any by themselves. There are benchmarks to hit, due dates for rough drafts, and word limits. If it is a science project, there will be requirements for the display. Students will have to buy a trifold.

It is a recipe for minimizing any chance the student might engage with the project. Thanks to technology, students nowadays often get new types of projects, usually using multimedia formats like movies, PowerPoint presentations, or MP3s. They might be asked to film their own version of the play they are reading, or pretend to be historical figures and declaim for a bit on historical events. They may be asked to make a coloring book for the human cell. These are more creative assessments, yes, and one can find these suggestions on hundreds of websites promising to enhance student motivation.

Nonetheless, these assignments still don't quite answer the most basic question teachers wrestle with every year when developing research projects: If the students don't really know the content, how are they supposed to come up with engaging questions? Armed with just a superficial understanding of the Great Depression, let's say, how should students know what interests them enough about it to be able to commit to a long-term investigation? And if they don't care enough about the topic to write an essay about it, why would they be more excited to film a movie about it instead?

The teacher needs to set up an entry point, this introduction to the project, in a way that leaves students with questions of their own devising and, without any real knowledge beyond what's right in front of their eyes, an intense desire to find the answers. What the teacher wants to do, of course, is to stimulate curiosity.

Teachers talk often about curiosity as a factor in learning—what it actually *is* is a matter of conjecture. Perceptual psychology refers to objects that catch the eye for the moment, usually because they are out of place—novelties in an overly familiar landscape. This interest fades rather quickly.

Epistemic curiosity is the sort of thing teachers are really looking to engender. It is a motivation to learn more caused by the realization that one's knowledge is incomplete. Moreover, it is suggested that the closer one comes to completing knowledge, the more one's desire to learn increases.

Conversely, too large of a gap is also dangerous. If a student knows nothing about a topic at all, there's no real point of entry. There's nothing for an epistemic curiosity to grab onto. George Lowenstein writes, "The information-gap perspective implies that awareness of an information gap is a necessary precondition for experiencing curiosity. Thus, a failure to appreciate what one does not know would constitute an absolute barrier to curiosity." In other words, students end up "Fat but Happy," a condition suggested by Charles Gettys in which "subjects have major knowledge gaps but are not aware of them."[1]

The Happy Meal idea has two benefits if this theory about curiosity is accurate. The Happy Meal is a relatively known substance. The students could be confronted by the need to create something completely novel—that is, remake a "slide rule challenge"—but if they have never seen a slide rule, the novelty will wear off without provoking much interest. Kids know about fast food, even if they don't eat at these restaurants. McDonald's alone spends nearly one billion a year on advertising.[2]

Kids likely also think they know more about fast food than they actually do, which is the second benefit of choosing the Happy Meal. It is better to have them overconfident. If pressed about what is actually in the food, or where it comes from, they will likely not know much more than some general concerns about artificial flavoring or cooking oil or perhaps GMOs. If doubly pressed by the need to recreate these components from scratch, they will soon find they know very little.

Great projects begin from simple starts. A fairly complex project requiring students to think about the way World War I shaped the 1920s and 1930s, especially with respect to the rise of German fascism, began simply with students telling stories about life-changing moments for themselves. Recognizing that the effects of events can linger long after they've happened led to increased empathy for an entire generation that clearly suffered from post-traumatic stress disorder.

The aquaponics project began with a trip to the port in Honolulu to watch container ships offloading the basic supplies Hawaiians needed that the islands couldn't furnish for them, and then a visit to a recycling center to watch great piles of stuff getting hauled to an incinerator. It finished with a community service trip to the University of Hawai'i lo'i, a naturally sustainable taro patch cultivated by ancient Hawaiian methods, where students first helped clear a stream of debris and then planted new taro shoots in the thick mud. The notions of ecological balance and disharmony were thus vividly rendered.

Of course, the simplest start for the UnHappy Meal project would be to have lunch. The third benefit of this project is that teenagers love to eat.

That said, novelty does create excitement in a way that simply dropping a sack of hamburgers on the table will not. If fast food itself is not thrilling (unless one is extremely hungry), creating a sense of drama around the opening event might throw the students off balance enough that this too-well-known item suddenly carries a hint of mystery. The proper frame of mind for the Unhappy Meal project is to assume one knows nothing, and therefore one doesn't quite know what to look for. That will be the surprise of discovery.

The hope therefore is to drop the students into the project in medias res—and hope the skills they have practiced to this point are enough to get their minds working. They will have to assess what they already know and what they need to know and if they or their prospective teammates have any transferable skills to help them rebuild the Happy Meal. They will have to practice seeing, thinking, and wondering about an object they have seen all their lives previously without seeing, thinking, or wondering about it in any particular way.

THE EVENT ITSELF

> Good entry events also convey a teacher's investment in the project. When teachers put their own creativity into launching a project, they share this unspoken message: We're about to embark on an important learning adventure together. Let's make it into a big deal.
> —Suzie Boss, "How to Get Projects Off to a Good Start"

What better to way to model deconstruction than by watching someone else deconstruct?

The students therefore began the entry event to the Unhappy Meal project by watching Thomas Thwaites's TED Talk about his Toaster Project. They needed to understand why the deconstruction and reconstruction of a basic object could be a rich and rewarding activity. As any good artist knows, humans have a fundamental lack of understanding of the items that they use every day. Therefore, everything around us is fundamentally strange, and worthy of closer notice—even the cheapest toaster on the shelf, as Thwaites learned.

The talk also offers the viewer an example of "raw inquiry," and the types of detours and surprises that might arise if one is determined enough to track things down to their source. One of the more fascinating aspects of his presentation is the realization that we have lost the technological ability to make even the simplest things entirely by hand—rather, we have become reliant on big industries employing economies of scale to mass produce cheaper items whose composition and point of origin has been obliterated. Thwaites at one point was reduced to thumbing through medieval texts in order to learn small-scale smelting.

A fairly famous (famous among science teachers, at any rate) documentary, *A Private Universe* (produced by the Harvard-Smithsonian Center for Astrophysics in 1987), depicts students graduating from Harvard failing to answer basic science questions correctly. From the origins of seasons to how a seed becomes a tree, or even why the moon has phases, these "brightest of their generation" could not either offer correct explanations or show a basic understanding of the terms they had been taught to use. They were confounded when introduced to their own ignorance.

Thus, prior to viewing Thwaites's TED Talk, the ninth graders were asked to explain how their favorite bits of technology actually worked. How does sound travel through cyberspace from their iPods to their wireless headphones? How do their parent's internal combustion engines work? What happens when they switch gears on their bikes? They probably couldn't do worse than the Harvard grads (admittedly, a low bar.) Hopefully, they'd be shocked by how little they knew about the objects they used daily.

Mr. Werberger's Teacher Journal

> I had set up them to fail, really. I referred to them as fine examples of Homo Technologicus, and praised them for being the most recent products of what had been a meteoric rise in technical knowledge for the human race. The silence that greeted my question was thus both profound and ironic. Only one student answered the questions about the transmission of sound. However, he used his phone to read from a description on Wikipedia. I asked him to explain the words he'd just read (which he mispronounced), but he admitted he couldn't. Nor could he explain how the answers appeared on his phone.
>
> I admitted these questions were unfair, especially, since I didn't know the answer either, and so I moved down to some more elemental questions.
>
> For instance—why does a ball stop rolling after you push it? Even though a few understood gravity and friction played a role, they didn't really know why or how. I went even more basic after that, asking them how their eyes saw color ("rods and cones!" they yelled, and others wanted to explain how we saw things upside down initially, but still couldn't explain how objects were constructed inside our brains from splashes of light and dark), what color even was, for that matter, and finally, what fire actually was and why it looked the way it did. Suffice to say, no one got close.
>
> Despite knowing how to use amazingly advanced technology, most of us are no better than cavemen, and probably less likely to get our simplest needs met if basic survival knowledge was required to do so.

Moreover, as *A Private Universe* suggests, students are more likely to retain misconceptions they had prior to learning the correct answers.

For the debrief I asked the students for one takeaway. Some were scared at about how reliant they realized they were on a few companies to make the things they needed, and others were surprised at how many different origins the toaster components had. They weren't that clear about why Thwaites did the project, though they guessed what was coming next and they seemed excited about the prospect of doing something similar. I just hadn't told them what that would be.

They figured it out, however, when our two buses pulled into a McDonald's. At first they thought I was buying them all lunch. I told them instead to take notes on what they saw in the "restaurant" while I ordered six Happy Meals. I was nonplussed to see they now offered milk (I was more interested in seeing them take apart soda), and a choice of apples or something called "GoGurt" as sides, though they still had the same burger and fries combo I was hoping for.

While I waited for the food to arrive, the students were busy taking pictures of people eating, or of the signage everywhere trumpeting the value options on the menu and the healthy choices McDonald's now offered. To their credit, the employees were perfectly friendly despite the explosion of ninth graders in their midst, and it took no more than ten minutes to get in and out of there. I did notice that a few students had managed to buy several orders of chicken nuggets, which they devoured on the way back to school.

UNMAKING

The task of deconstruction is fundamental for both the sciences and the arts. The elemental task of Western science seems to have been to dismantle substances down to the smallest particle in order to reconstruct how everything around us actually works. This is sometimes called "reverse engineering."

The overlap of this approach to the humanities is evident in how much of modern literary theory speaks of deconstructing the text in order to extract meaning. Many of the most recent advances in pedagogy have come from neuroscientists deconstructing the human brain, or at least isolating the geographies of its various functions.

STEM education often features this basic task of knowing through division. Mark, a STEM teacher in Hawai'i, described an activity called the "Sludge Test" that he once ran in an introductory science course for freshman. Several different versions of this exist from just a cursory Internet search, but its essence is that several different chemicals are mixed in a bottle, and the students are expected to use several different testing methods to separate and identify the ingredients of this dark, gooey, sludgy matter.

The students are not only given concrete lessons in chemical distillation, but the purpose for doing them is made clear in the process. The object of their study is visible, tangible, and unknown—inquiry and investigation makes it known to them. More important, the actual deconstruction itself is the focus of inquiry. The deconstruction is itself the test, really. This is a perfect encapsulation of science as a method for knowing the world.

Says Mark, "You spend the first part of the course having kids do performance task activities around understanding matter—boiling point, solubility, density, and so on. The culminating task is [the Sludge test]. What I loved about the test is that the essential question is simple—'What is matter made of?'" One of the first challenges was to distill wood. "The students heat it up until it is deconstructed into solids (carbon), liquids, and gasses. It blows kids' minds when they realize all those substances were in a piece of wood. . . . Every activity is always pointing back to the essential question."

What might that look like in a classroom that is not, in fact, an arts class? Perhaps something that is ostensibly a ninth-grade history course?

The students are handed a "memory box" that is filled with photographs, postcards, stamps, and a few handwritten notes. The contents show mustachioed white men in pith hats and late Victorian safari wear. They are shown in various scenarios—boarding steamships laden with ivory, overseeing dark-skinned laborers pounding the sap from trees, riding bicycles or lounging in hammocks while being fanned by the same dark-skinned laborers. Here and there, a note refers to notions of power, of trade, of "civilizing the natives," while other notes speak of the cruelties imposed on the local people—whippings, hangings, and the amputation of hands.

The students investigate the images, asking questions based on these details and their own hypotheses. Their explorations take them to the Belgian Congo, to King Leopold and Joseph Conrad, to Roger Casement and his extensive reportage on the depredations of colonialism. Digging further, the students must tackle the wealth of secondary information that exists in order to evaluate the claims of the Belgian imperial agents versus the reformers who sought to stop them. They look beyond the immediacy of the era, hoping to understand the motive for colonialism and then leaping ahead to see its effects to better evaluate what happened.

Their test is to build a case by collating this information, evaluating their sources, and constructing a story that establishes force and agency, narrates cause and effect, and navigating bias and perspective. This is how history is done by the professionals, after all—by sifting through the randomness of the available evidence to construct a fiction that satisfies the human need to understand.

But what about the human need to create?

UNMAKING AND REMAKING

An interesting twist on the Sludge Test, therefore, might be to require the students who pass it to design the sludge for the incoming students. Might the process of recreating the test—and even improving on its complexity—be a better test of knowledge? What if the challenge was extended to create a "Sludge of Another Color"? For the history class, similarly, perhaps the students should create a new memory box—but this time, based on their interests, not those of the teacher. They must deconstruct a story they know well and construct a test that will allow another student to develop the skills to recreate it.

Is here is an analogous step for artists, a deconstruction of other works that provides both a thorough grounding in the application of technique and the instigation for a new creation? After all, what is the intent when a jazz musician digs into *The Great American Songbook*, or a filmmaker creates an homage in their movie to a previous director? What goes on in the process of reconstructing a version of the thing deconstructed?

Andy, a musician, says, "The essence of jazz is to take a song heard hundreds of times before—say, a trio plays 'Julia' by the Beatles . . . it's [chosen on] a whim. It depends on where you are at the time emotionally or contextually. It's partly for the audience, as well. It's comfort food." However, Nikki, a visual artist, adds that she will dissect other works, or assign her students to do so, because in her words, "It's good to see what mastery looks like as a starting point. It's not just imitation, but hopefully inspiration. How is the work I'm viewing adding to a discussion that already exists?"

Art challenges both the artist and the audience to find the unexpected in what is already known, and then to understand where both the maker and viewer exist in relation to it. It is the essence of epistemic curiosity. One imagines that the difference in art lies, much as with sports, in the question "How do I do that myself," rather than just "How does that work?"

Therefore, if that's the starting point, what does the subsequent process of creation look like? Both say the new piece or version will be shaped by conscious or subconscious influences—it's an echo of the older work or a response to it. Andy says that his jazz trio will play a popular song slower or in a more dynamic way depending on where they are in the set. "Sometimes we start all together, and someone will start playing something slightly different, and we all go in another direction entirely. We don't always come back."

In a similar way, Nikki says that she sees the concept behind an existing piece of work as "scaffolding to use it for something else. Someone who uses space outside the frame . . . the idea is what's interesting—not the content itself. The existing work is a palette to 'freak out on.'"

The Happy Meal, similarly, will challenge the students to see what a version of mastery is—the ability to mass produce food for billions of consumers—but will hopefully challenge them to see something unusual in what they had previously thought of as food. And the ultimate lure, again, is the chance to see how they can make that themselves—to riff on a theme—not just to understand how it's made.

For this purpose, the conditions of the Sludge Test were recreated. The students brought the meals back to a biology classroom and laid them on top of butcher paper. They were instructed to break each part of the meal down to its constituent parts—to go as small as possible without having to resort to special equipment.

An additional challenge was to deconstruct things like mustard packets down their raw components. They solved this partly by reading the ingredients list on the package, but this was mostly confusing, as even the apple slices contained chemicals they neither recognized nor understood.

For record keeping, they were asked to draw a mind-web of every component of each part, and how everything fit in relation with everything else. Think of it as something like the blueprint of an Ikea bedframe. Then they each began to identify the components they found more curious than the others, and developed questions about them that further developed that initial curiosity into a proper investigation.

Mr. Werberger's Teacher Journal

This led to some fairly interesting paths of inquiry I hadn't anticipated—but then again, I wasn't sure what to expect, anyway. But several students who were becoming disturbed at the sheer amount of all the chemical preservatives listed in the packaging wondered what would happen if they burned the food. Others wondered how long it actually takes for the various bits to decompose if left somewhere unmolested over time. Two science teachers who had been coopted for this activity agreed to facilitate some experiments, but they made the students develop hypotheses and guidelines before they could go ahead with their plans.

Soon, there were several Bunsen burners going, or bits of meat and bread being placed into petri dishes. Watching the grease drip from the fries as they carbonized made several students swear off them for the foreseeable future. The students worked hard for hours on this, and only lost steam with about ten minutes to go. The vegetarians and vegans meanwhile looked smug, especially as the classroom began to take on a noticeably "off" odor.

I left the class with a debrief blog to write, in which I asked them to discuss, individually, a list of things they had to have or learn to do in order to recreate the Happy Meal. This was to be followed by a list of

questions they wanted to investigate, including any questions they
wanted to direct to Thomas Thwaites, the Toaster Project guy.

The final step was to list her or his skills or any special knowledge that
could come in handy in this project. These could be related to making
the physical components, managing the project, research and investigation, or creating social media to talk about the project, and so on.

Johann: What's in a Happy Meal? Pretty easy, right? Just like a hamburger, fries, a drink, apples, you know the stuff. But when you actually look at the fine print you see a lot more.

There're too many ingredients. I mean, like, there is a lot of stuff in
those things. There is a lot of stuff that we don't think about to make all
this food addictive, each piece carefully analyzed to see if it increased
sales or did not.

I'm super pumped for a project like this. Although that sounds like I'm
a sixth grader who just got an award for participation, this project
actually interests me. First, this whole thing is crazy to think about. It's
basically who can manufacture something best with their hands. Now,
I have no doubt if Ron Swanson was participating he would win, but
it's almost like a survival challenge, mixed with the intuition of a high
school, combined with top chef. I mean, that sounds pretty badass to
me.

Part of the excitement over this project is the idea that this has never
even occurred to me. Basically, this whole week has been a complete
"open up" moment in class, we learned about a possible book, and
what we're actually doing. Once I actually realized what we were doing, I got really excited, which has a brother that usually follows along
with it, fear.

I could go on and on about what could go wrong. The "What Ifs" and
the "Buts," and I could actually bring up some pretty good points. But
from previous assignments and from plenty of projects with others, I
learned that you really need to be careful who you put your trust in.
The concern that really scares me is working with others, I don't have a
problem working with others, but putting my trust in them to get them
to accomplish things, I have a problem with. Have you ever worked
your ass off on a project, and your "partner" didn't meet the deadline,
or didn't work to help out, or had a really crappy part to theirs, which
brought down yours? All. The. Time.

To be blunt, I'll work if I'm interested. If this thing really gets a grip on
me, I will go all out. And this thing has me really into it. I feel like I
could really do something with this project, and take something out of
the whole experience. I can direct people pretty easily, sheeple are
something that everybody has to deal with eventually. As for resources, I just need access to the locations where we get these materials.
I'll need the basic equipment to create things like this, because I'm
pretty sure we aren't building printers, but we are creating the ink. I

feel like the best way to do this is step-by-step, but each person having their own step.

Where do we start? What is the first step, and what is our first goal? What order do we create the pieces in, since they're food, they will eventually go bad. These are the first questions I would ask when determining how we'll do this project. I'm super excited to see where this takes the class, and pray that we can actually accomplish this.

Cady: I like this project because of the weirdness. Seriously, how many teachers excuse their students from three classes, drive them to McDonald's, tell them to take notes on people while not looking like stalkers, and let them eat their research? Maybe it's just me but all of those are all firsts. It's also a little crazy because it's so new. Seven months sounds like a lot of work. I don't know what's happening in seven minutes. Seven months is pretty much unfathomable.

I think I could be useful in this experiment because I like to cook and bake. I'm not sure if I would call reconstructing McDonald's meals cooking but it does sound interesting. I am curious to discover what exactly goes into McDonald's food. It's like I want to look away but I can't. It's grossly fascinating. I especially want to know about the vegetable products like the apples and the French fries. I want to know how much is real vegetable and how much is artificial filling or who knows what. It's a little creepy to think that I have no clue what I'm putting in my mouth half the time.

NOTES

1. George Loewenstein, "The Psychology of Curiosity: A Review and Reinterpretation," *Psychological Bulletin* 116, no. 1 (1994: 75–90), https://www.cmu.edu/dietrich/sds/docs/loewenstein/PsychofCuriosity.pdf.

2. Scott Hume, "McDonald's Spent More Than 988 Million on Advertising in 2013," *Christian Science Monitor,* March 30, 2014, http://www.csmonitor.com/Business/The-Bite/2014/0330/McDonald-s-spent-more-than-988-million-on-advertising-in-2013.

FIVE

Deconstruction of Self

Any assessment model contains an inherent flaw—to quantify "learning" confines it to what is being assessed. If a third party—the teacher, the state, College Board—creates the assessment, there will always ultimately be a disconnect between the student and the test. Educators spend far too much time convincing students why tests matter and that success on them equals "learning." In the end, tests likely only measure test taking. Information becomes merely the means to an end, and that which is deemed relevant is only so because the third party has declared it to be.

It is stunning how quickly details that amaze and delight children become dull and uninteresting once it has been quantified in the higher grades. At some point, education becomes as much a matter of knowing the right words as truly knowing what those words mean. "Photosynthesis," "cosine," "popular sovereignty"—these are all fascinating, complex concepts that every high school student is expected to understand, but which seem to exist only as abstract definitions. Knowing is not understanding. If students could play with these concepts, subvert them, *dance* them—that would be true comprehension.

One way of giving the student control over the assessment and the means to create something unique and self-expressive might be to blend the arts into engineering and the sciences. Yet to truly embrace the possibilities of spontaneity and divergent thinking, perhaps an educator could put the weight of their focus on the arts as an approach to learning—not an addition to learning. In this model, a test or a performance does not mean the learning is over; a test is only a snapshot of a moment along the true journey, a chance to reflect on where the student is and how much farther they need to go.

Traditional testing, no matter how imaginative, places the student outside of what is being studied. It also refuses to acknowledge the role the test maker plays in distorting what is supposed to be "true." It assumes knowledge is static. Arts-based research embraces dynamism and flow. It blurs the line between learner and subject. It assumes that the learner is shaping knowledge both by observing it and by communicating what is learned. It is improvisational and requires the artist-researcher to be constantly adaptive in their interactions with subject audience.

This project was an attempt to teach self-awareness and improvisational thinking in a ninth-grade classroom. The students were encouraged to become "beautifully lost," to see their environment as unfamiliar—and then to understand why and how they had gotten that way. In a way, they were instructed to listen for their voice, to understand how their choices and their tools had led them to an impasse. They were being taught to think of themselves as the most proper object of study, which is the first principle of philosophy. Their final assessment was to explain their own conclusions about themselves.

DECONSTRUCTION IS A PATH TO SELF-KNOWLEDGE

Once the Happy Meals had been deconstructed, the students were going to have to figure out how to put them back together again—but not as McDonald's made them. This project was an exercise in learning the technical proficiency to make food, but also for making something uniquely personal to each student out of this food a statement about politics, about ethics, about passion. It was to be a blend of art and science, but how could the classroom be a place where poetic and scientific thinking were not just co-taught, but co-mingled?

The stereotype of the scientist is of the researcher in the white coat, testing and retesting data to come as close to objective view of the as possible. The stereotype of the artist? Someone in a paint-smeared smock, smashing shibboleths and rejecting a cold, dispassionate objective view of the world. It is likely that the scientist and the artist have a quite similar goal in mind, though their methods might veer. The purpose of this project is ultimately to suggest that the methods employed by the artist to know the world have as much as or more validity to a ninth-grade student learning via history or science.

The process of creation does not seem linear. Its essence is that is open to possibilities that were not expected. Creativity is a method for engendering constant surprise. It seems recursive in that an artist is constantly referring the work of creation back to themselves—*where am I in this process, what am I trying to say, is this work saying what I want it to say?* Work can be abandoned without loss, since it is not the work that matters, but the thinking that goes into it.

Learning is not necessarily linear, either. Learning is a desire to know, and it creates new needs as more and more is learned. Yet it is based on curiosity, and curiosity is capricious. Our desires may stem from an immediate whim or a long-nurtured passion, or be dropped as suddenly as it came. It is also recursive. It is a process of fitting in what we now know with what we already knew, and thinking further about what remains to be known. Like play, it is often purposeful, but not always teleological. It may not always have a clear purpose or use.

To link learning with creativity means we will have to learn to see what we choose not to notice. We must be able to observe ourselves as we construct our own meaning. It means reconsidering the purpose of learning, and the measurement by which we can know whether we have learned. This may mean rethinking everything we assume we know about the high school classroom, but the stakes seem worth it.

By understanding how we learn, we can understand ourselves.

WHAT IS THE DANGER OF TELEOLOGICAL THINKING?

In any discussion about pedagogy, which usually becomes an argument about the most effective form of teaching, assessment is the 900-pound gorilla in the room. How does one quantify student learning, or prove one particular approach is the best, without some form of evaluation? Education without assessment is almost unimaginable. Even students who have every reason to hate testing and grades regard a school without them with suspicion.

Prelesson testing reveals what the students don't yet know about a topic, just-in-time quizzing shows what they learned from last night's reading, summative testing shows what they have learned thus far. Diagnostic testing shows the students' strengths as learners, or the challenges they must overcome. PSATs, SATs, and ACTs quantify the overall effect of all their schooling to help colleges cull the ranks of applicants—or even determine a teacher's "merit." Tests, tests, and more tests.

The logical consequence of our educational system's current approach to testing is the belief that metadata, as analyzed by a body of experts, can help these same experts design an educational system that will raise America's competitiveness with the rest of the world, at least according to the tests they design to measure this. As a result, more and more school systems become organized around these tests, which are happening at earlier ages and with more frequency.

This has of course engendered resistance in the form of the "opt-out" movement, in which parents and students in several states, including New York, Illinois, and Washington, have declared war on excessive testing. Teachers have some of their own reasons for opposing testing, especially in the wake of legislative measures that tie their pay or their job security to signs of improvement in student scores.

However, the most common complaint teachers make about test-based education is the degree to which the test dictates the course of learning in the classroom. This is true whether a classroom is geared toward making gains on SATs or making 4s and 5s on subject-specific AP tests. Knowing the types of questions on these tests or the general areas that must be covered will inherently dictate the material that is to be taught and how it will be assessed.

AP teachers thus find themselves forced to ensure the target areas are covered appropriately, at the cost of a more leisurely and tangential foray through their subject material. Math is now taught during English classes when math scores are low, and reading is taught in math when those scores need to be raised. Public school teachers spend their summers learning the new assessment models, and spend the year retraining their students to take them. The nature of education now is that if data is not quantifiable, it isn't worth looking at it.

The question is, is there a purpose to this type of education beyond success on the cumulative exam? It appears that standardized testing measures only how well students take standardized exams. Educational companies make a lot of money selling supplemental materials for their own tests. They have created perfect synergy for themselves, and have become a powerful enough lobbying force to have their business model legislated into the schools.[1] Many universities—800 at last count—appear to have realized the circuitous nature of the industry and are beginning to drop or make standardized score reporting optional.[2]

Standardized testing has, at any rate, been questioned by educational reformers for its accuracy since the first tests were instituted. The larger question therefore is to what degree does *any* assessment distort the learning process?

All tests must, by their definition, impose linear instruction. Learning becomes teleological—designed to an end in mind. Even tests that are meant to measure nonlinear thinking must assume that instruction geared toward facilitating nonlinear thinking has either occurred or not occurred.

The College Work Readiness Assessment (CWRA) is an example of a standardized test that quantifies the students ability to read several sources on a given, usually nonacademic, topic and create a unique argument from them. For instance, a student might be given a table of statistics on deaths from smoking, an extract from a scientific paper on second-hand smoke, some open letters to the editor, and a PR handout from a tobacco company, and then is asked to weigh in on a law banning smoking in public venues. The student writes a response that synthesizes the documents and gets points for their ability to analyze their usefulness in parsing the argument.

As explained on the Council for Aid to Education's website, the CWRA is open-ended with respect to the student's response, but not to their ability to:

- "assert a logical decision or conclusion and support it with appropriate information from the Document Library,
- construct organized and logically cohesive arguments,
- strengthen their position by elaborating on facts or ideas, and
- demonstrate facility with the conventions of standard written English."[3]

This raises an interesting logical question: Can a test maker create a test that does not, by its own internal requirements or the course it shapes for the teachers, commit the basic fallacy of presumption? Presumption is the process of building an argument backward from a truth one is ostensibly trying to prove, but which is assumed to be true from the beginning. It begins with an a priori assumption whose veracity is never questioned, and ends with the assumption being proved by the reasoning process.

A classic example might occur in a history class, in which the causes of the American Revolution are laid out in a reasonable fashion over a few weeks, and at the end, the students are tested on their ability to explain the causes of the revolution. In other words, the revolution is an established fact that occurs in an established timeline, and the study of the revolution in class consistently reaffirms its existence. Students are evaluated on their ability to reaffirm the existence of an event that is already acknowledged to have happened and to restate it according to the pattern experts have already told them is the correct one to identify.

A problem with this approach has already been discussed—there is little room for student curiosity or emotional involvement with a preselected topic for which there is little range for interpretation. This is why books promising to restore student motivation remain bestsellers year after year. It is also why students are periodically given a break from reading and lectures and told to draw a picture of the main character/ historical theme/scientific object—just for fun!

A second, more conceptual problem, however, is that there is some evidence that the way humans create stories from cause and effect is more a matter of brain structure than anything occurring in nature. Humans like to impose order on random events, and one way we do that is by weeding out a lot of the background noise in order to show a simplified schematic of relationships between a handful of significant events. Students learn that the French and Indian War "caused" the American Revolution, for example, in order to create some logical pattern to help students make sense of the chaos. In other words, the entire premise of K-12 history classes may be a useful fiction.[4]

Science suffers from the logical inconsistencies wrought by presumption as well. Researchers are prone to cherry picking evidence that proves a hypothesis correct, or of discarding aberrant information that doesn't fit a desired pattern. Thomas Kuhn famously illustrated the degree to which scientists are willing to overlook blatantly contradictory evidence in support of a model they feel comfortable with.

Even Gregor Mendel, the very model of scientific thinking according to high school textbooks, appears to have, perhaps unconsciously, tossed out evidence that didn't fit within the ratios he needed to explain the occurrence of physical characteristics in his pea plants. A much more deliberate fraud was committed by early proponents of race-based neuroscience, as detailed by Stephen Jay Gould in his *Mismeasure of Man*. Tests were consciously rigged in order to prove not just the supremacy of whites, but of a certain kind of white—specifically, the whites who had concocted the theory of white supremacy.

An interesting application of this phenomenon appeared in *Retraction Watch* in 2013 in which David Vaux discussed his attempt to retract his own article from *Nature* after he was unable to replicate the results from that article. *Nature* appears to have refused to retract the article, but did print a redacted version of his own retraction, and thus, the flawed evidence still remains in print today.

He adds, "The retraction was published in 1998, and has attracted 16 citations of its own. However, of the 976 citations of the Bellgrau et al. paper, about 700 were subsequent to publication of the retraction, so it's clear many remain unaware that its findings are questionable. Clearly, the processes that allow the scientific record to self-correct can be improved, not least by *Nature*."[5]

Sigmund Freud, whose own work has come under suspicion for rigging conclusions, had this to say to would-be researchers in 1912:

> It is not a good thing to work on a case scientifically while treatment is still proceeding—to piece together its structure, to try to foretell its further progress. . . . as scientific interest would demand. Cases which are devoted from the first to scientific purposes and are treated accordingly suffer in their outcome; while the most successful cases are those in which one proceeds, as it were, without any purpose in view, allows oneself to be taken by surprise by any new turn in them, and always meets them with an open mind, free from presuppositions.[6]

There is a danger in assuming that learning is teleological and that it is linear. The danger is that one will tend to prove what one believes already to be true, and that the answers are true and always have been. Evidence that is contrary or doesn't fit the story will be ignored for the sake of keeping the accepted story accurate. A more interesting test would be one, therefore, that incorporated surprise, and which, in Freud's words, encourages students encountering surprises to "meet them with an open mind, free from presuppositions."

One attempt to encourage this, especially in the sciences, has been the idea of STEAM (Science, Technology, Engineering, Arts, Mathematics) education.

THE MARRIAGE OF THE ARTS AND SCIENCES

The Rhode Island School of Design and National Science Foundation collaborated in 2011 to popularize STEAM—that is, adding the arts, with its emphasis on design, divergent thinking, and play, to engineering classes. Its proponents, among which are several blue-chip industries, say, "the arts hold great potential to foster creativity and new ways of thinking that can help unleash STEM innovation." The benefits to said industries are obvious.

A typical STEAM project might be to paint a reproduction of a cell, or to create artwork using mathematically ordered shapes. The goal of many such projects seems to be to take content knowledge and find imaginative ways of reproducing it, thus giving the student a chance to have a unique voice in showing what they have learned. Additionally, the role of the arts seems to be a way to hook students into learning content material that might otherwise seem dry and uninteresting.

The more ambitious proponents claim that the arts must have their own rigorous epistemologies that can only enhance the work that scientists do. The article mentions a 2008 Michigan State study that discovered "Nobel laureates in the sciences were 22 times more likely than scientists in general to be involved in the performing arts."

An Ohio art teacher who collaborated on the cell watercolor project at the Dayton Regional STEM School found that her way of making work bore quite a bit in common with the way her partners in the science department made theirs. "One thing we looked at . . . was how artists and scientists have common methodologies in observing the world around them."[7]

This suggests an interesting take on STEAM: Why not start with the arts and add science, math, history, and language to it? Or better, why not just call all of it "The Arts"?

Stanford University Arts and Education professor Eliot Eisner was a leading proponent of using the arts not to add creativity to an existing science or history project, but rather, of using the arts as a thinking process to teach history or science. As he suggested in his 1982 *Cognition and Curriculum*, one's sensorial experience in confronting the object of study was just as important as rational thinking in education. All the senses are involved in making meaning from what is being examined. He thus argued that learning environments should be immersive and personal to the student.

The corollary to this is that communicating what has been learned is also immersive and personal, since the same senses used to learn are used to communicate. He advocated that students should seek multiple venues of self-expression, some without words, some with symbols of the student's own devising. This is where imagination and creativity enter— as the means for students to show their own understanding, not to repeat back the teacher's understanding.

The greater goal of this kind of education is not merely to know the outside world. It is, rather, for the students to know themselves. As he later wrote, "This is, perhaps, the largest lesson that the arts in education can teach, the lesson that life itself can be led as a work of art. In so doing the maker himself or herself is remade. The remaking, this re-creation is at the heart of the process of education."[8]

Shaun McNiff further defines this approach to learning:

> Perhaps a defining quality of art-based researchers is their willingness to start the work with questions and a willingness to design methods in response to the particular situation, as contrasted to the more general contemporary tendency within the human sciences to fit the question into a fixed research method. The art of the art-based researcher extends to the creation of a process of inquiry.[9]

In other words, an artist might create small pieces of work in immediate response to a set of stimuli—the human cell, the flow of water, a collection of poems—and then examine those pieces of art to see if a pattern emerges that leads to a focused inquiry. Or, those pieces of art might be shown to an audience to elicit feedback from observers.

The notion of "arts-based research" therefore becomes compelling, as it offers a way for students to study the world, but to do so in a way that stresses adaptability and improvisation in addition to deep focus and attention to details. Moreover, it acknowledges the role of the observer's own presence and engagement with the object of study. In that respect, it seems more honest than scientific disciplines that lay claim to a disinterested objectivity, which is rarely true.

In a sense, the student in an art-based research classroom would learn not only the content and skills of the subject at hand, but might, by a similar process of deconstruction—by thinking more deeply about the kinds of questions they are asking, or the topics they find interesting within that field—deconstruct themselves as well. The classroom must be open to improvisation—the sudden twists and turns that students will make as the focus of their curiosity changes.

WHAT IS IMPROVISATIONAL THINKING?

It makes sense to start this section by talking about jazz. Jazz is an act of improvisation. Its history and culture are bound up with a disdain for rules and constraints. Its heroes were masters of playing around the melodies of the songs they covered, changing keys and tempos to express alterations of mood. Their highly individualistic solos were their way to communicate their thoughts, their identities, to the audience. Creativity mattered as much as skill. To be unique was to be all.

Charles Limb, a professor at Johns Hopkins School of Medicine, and a musician says, "When jazz musicians improvise, they often play with eyes closed in a distinctive, personal style that transcends traditional rules of melody and rhythm. It's a remarkable frame of mind during which, all of a sudden, the musician is generating music that has never been heard, thought, practiced or played before. What comes out is completely spontaneous."[10]

Several recent studies have been undertaken to understand why and how improvisation happens. What has become clear is that improvisation is a form of thinking all its own, and one that has a broadly holistic effect on the overall brain. Improvising does not arise from a disdain for the rational. It may be the most supremely rational cognitive act we are capable of. It is also perhaps a tool that figures largely in human evolution.

One study began, oddly enough, after a cognitive ethnomusicologist named Aaron Berkowitz watched classical pianist Robert Levin improvise on the great works of Mozart and Beethoven. While a stereotype of classical music is that its excellence is partly determined by its adherence to the composer's own score, improvisation in classical music is not atypical, as it turns out. Mozart and Beethoven often made up parts of their scores on the spot, and Liszt worked audience suggestions into his performances, although he never played them as given.

Levin, who also teaches music at Harvard, says that improvisation is a means of communication between the performer and the audience, and that the danger of failure—of beginning an act of creativity that could fail, heightens the drama for the spectator and creates a personal bond with the musician. A concert therefore becomes less of a passive exercise, and more of a lived experience. What Levin could not explain is where this talent comes from—is it intuitive, or a learned skill?

Berkowitz's theory was that music was much like language. As children learn to speak, they begin by learning phrases by rote memorization, and as fluency increases, the ability to play with language arises as these imprinted bits are recombined in the brain to express new ideas. Whether musician or poet, Berkowitz suggests that the artist becomes both creator and observer, sometimes surprised by what comes out but able to consciously adapt it to the flow.

To examine this further, Berkowitz and his partner, Daniel Ansari, developed an experiment wherein the test subjects, all classically trained musicians, played a variety of pieces—from rote to freestyle—while having their brains mapped by externally placed magnets that measure blood flow to various parts of the brain. Their initial findings showed that three distinct regions all lit up during the more improvisational tasks, and each region plays its own cognitive role in helping us navigate daily life.

As had expected, one area that lit up during the test is that same that enables us to create and comprehend language. A second locus, the dorsal premotor cortex, helps the body move within perceived space and develop a plan of action. The third region, the anterior cingulate, is the one we use when trying to deal with conflicting stimuli. This region helps us avoid being distracted while we try to focus on the task at hand.

In other words, improvisation relies on deep concentration, rather than some ethereal, God-given talent for stringing random pieces of data together harmonically. It is when we improvise that we are in our fiercest focus.[11]

Charles Limb and his partner Allen Braun conducted a similar test meant to discover how the whole brain is affected by creative thinking. They found that one section of the prefrontal cortex of the brain, which can be likened to our "voice of restraint," goes on hiatus while musicians are improvising. Another section of the prefrontal cortex, which is our "autobiographical" locus—the place where we express ourselves and otherwise convey our individuality, fires up.

Limb says, "Jazz is often described as being an extremely individualistic art form. You can figure out which jazz musician is playing because one person's improvisation sounds only like him or her. What we think is happening is when you're telling your own musical story, you're shutting down impulses that might impede the flow of novel ideas. . . . Without this type of creativity, humans wouldn't have advanced as a species. It's an integral part of who we are."[12]

A corroborative study by Oded Kleinmintz et al., poses a dialectic between the creation of ideas and the brain's attempt to evaluate them. They tested musicians and nonmusicians in a brainstorming exercise that asked participants to develop divergent uses for common objects and then to rank the ideas by their range of deviance from high to low. They found that musicians outperformed nonmusicians, but that improvisational musicians also outperformed nonimprovisational musicians in their output.

Moreover, improvisers have a greater tolerance for ideas that might be considered too deviant by nonimprovisers. Self-imposed inhibition, or the "evaluation of ideas," may both prelimit the total number of ideas developed, and certainly imposes a limit on those ideas that were developed. They conclude:

> As humans, our first behaviors are improvisational in nature. Through learning we may also put more and more restrictions and inhibitions on different aspects of our lives. According to this idea, it is possible that musicians who do not practice improvisation actually practice/

train not to improvise and or to be creative in an improvisatory way. These nonimprovisers try to apply practice, knowledge and inhibition, whereas improvisers try to forsake these practiced known habits after they were properly learned.

Accordingly, the effect of training that involves decreasing the activity of the evaluation system may be to increase creative output. . . . [T]he implications of these findings should be considered in professional as well as educational settings to see how students can be taught to evaluate without compromising their creative products. [13]

Thus, we come again to the notion that teleological thinking, or, constraining oneself to a narrow range of solutions before even beginning to answer the problem—the basis for most middle and high school education—may actually thwart the pursuit of higher cognitive abilities in our students by inhibiting divergent thinking and also the holistic meta-functioning of our brains.

WHAT DOES ALL THIS MEAN FOR A HIGH SCHOOL TEACHER?

The arts are often used in schools as a way to get students to be more excited about science, math, and history—excited about the possibility of adding an element of creativity and personalization to what is often considered abstracted details and rote memorization. If one changes the perception that the arts exist mostly as a means of self-expression and consider them instead as a way of knowing the world that is just as rigorous and challenging as any other epistemology, a very different set of opportunities open up for the teacher.

The arts are a way to for a student to not just use creativity but to learn to *be* creative.

The arts are a way not to simply encourage students to study a topic, but as a tool to *learn* the topic.

The arts are a way for the students to not just express themselves, but to be aware of how they have to come to know what they want to say.

The arts are a way for students to achieve greater focus and concentration while learning, and yet to allow themselves to embrace divergent thinking by inhibiting themselves less. They are a way to balance the brain.

The arts are a framework on which to hang that content and those skills we insist they practice so that they become more efficient improvisers and more adaptive thinkers. That is, they can learn, through practice, to become more open to innovation.

The arts are a way the students can take risks in their learning, so long as their performance is assessed on the risks they take and not solely on the rightness of their answers.

Yet what it looks like to try this in one's own classroom is a bit foggy. It's hard to imagine how a teacher can prepare to lead an improvisational classroom. For instance, if fluency with improvisation arises once all the tools have been repeated to the point they can be used without conscious effort, does this mean a student should simply memorize all the data in a history textbook to be improvise historically? It's a grim picture.

Moreover, even if a teacher could create a classroom that was inherently improvisational, that afforded the students the maximum of intellectual freedom, it would thus be even harder to come with a list of guidelines and practices for another teacher. One cannot truly manage chaos. The question is again—how to teach something that seems innate? It is perhaps best to offer an example of how embracing improvisational thinking solved one particular problem with the research-based stage of the Unhappy Meal project.

The deconstruction of the Happy Meals had just ended and the students had begun to fall into self-assigned roles, in preparation of reconstruction, based on their interests. That is, some had become curious about the packaging—why there was so much of it, for one thing, but also how substitutes could be made organically. Others wondered about the meat—how we would get it, mostly. They were all interested in how food could be kept on the shelf for so long and still have it look mostly like food.

The teacher felt that this was the time to begin a round of research dedicated to the rebuilding process, and in this way, address an issue that had begun to arise with the students' work. After three months of investigation and writing prior to the UnHappy Meal introduction, the students had begun to fall into old routines. They had stopped validating their sources or exploring their purpose of their questions, and instead, had gotten used to coming up with a handful of facts that related to their investigation topic and stopping there as though a meaningful answer had been created. In short, they had gotten bored and were taking shortcuts.

It's so easy to get sucked into the routine of schoolwork, of falling into the trap of continuing the same assessments as before even when the purposes have changed. The teacher was still thinking of research as *answers* to questions, and the research ended when the questions had been answered in enough detail. As a result, the details become slowly fetishized over the questions. If inquiry was the focus of the classroom, he slowly realized he needed assessments that focused on the questions themselves, and not the information collected in response.

The students had fallen away from working with a self-directed purpose or embracing the unknown of investigation. They had become satisfied with facile responses to their complex investigations. How could they understand that real learning is not linear but embraces swerves as old questions are abandoned and new problems encountered? How could they understand that a question easily answered is perhaps not a useful one?

To this end, a rather long and thorough investigation model was constructed for this new research assignment, in which every step of research would be worked through elaborately and with opportunities for student "play," conversation, and critique. Each step of the process had a day devoted to it and at least one activity, with models to deconstruct and artifacts to create and post for discussion.

On Day 1, the students read a short article in common and collaborated on a "See, Think, Wonder" exercise to develop Essential Questions (EQs). They sat in their project teams with a stack of Post-it® notes and were asked to write down facts or statements that seem curious, interesting, or important and stick their notes on the table—a low-tech model of a Google Doc.

They then organized their Post-it notes into groups by theme or similarity, developing summary statements and hypotheses that explained the linkage of these facts or provided some insight into the importance and meaning of the facts (why these were chosen, for example). Each student was asked to develop at least one EQ from those hypotheses.

On the second day, they worked on creating "research declarations." That is a paragraph—almost like a journal abstract—that lays out the EQ, why the student is asking the question, and then requires the students to develop a series of smaller questions, more factually based questions that must be investigated to answer the big question.

The EQ was not really the point of the investigation. A good one is unlikely to be answerable at any rate, at least at a high school level. "How do we feed the world?" is a great question, but even PhDs struggle to respond well to it. The smaller questions, the ones that lead to concrete, testable ideas, were "what is the minimum that people need to eat to survive? What kinds of foods produce the most yields for the least resources? Is surplus food produced anywhere? How much does it cost to ship it somewhere else?" Those are the ones that matter if you are assessing the student's ability to find information and think about it.

On the third day, the students played games with web resources to gauge whether the source was a valid one for their purposes by looking at the author's credentials, the purpose of the site, whether the information was sourced to another article or database, and so on. They also critiqued each other's source assessments, and then debated back and forth on the trustworthiness of suspect sources. In some cases the students agreed they hadn't thought critically enough about a source since it had conveniently answered their questions, while others passionately defended their choices despite their peers' objections.

The fourth day required them to begin using those sources to collect details in response to their investigation questions. This is the moment where the problem of linear thinking would arise. Information gathering seems to be a solitary endeavor for students, even with the sort of benchmarks teachers create to keep them on track, and it's a temptation to switch over to autopilot and just skim for data that immediately fits into the outline.

How does one create the opportunity for students to play with data, to improvise and adapt, in a way consonant with what we have seen possible with arts-based research?

Mr. Werberger's Teacher Journal

I initially imagined that the students would read and annotate away until their questions had been resolved in some way, but I ran into two complications that actually provided me a breakthrough in rethinking the entire purpose of research projects.

The students kept asking if they could change their questions as their interests shifted—something that always occurs in the research process, but which in the past I had always cautioned students against doing. Something about capital already expended, and the cost of redoing an entire line of inquiry after so much effort and so little time remaining. . . . This time, I saw an opportunity for the kids to practice divergent thinking, and so I encouraged these new directions each time, as long as they could make it clear to me in their writing why they had changed topics.

Second, I watched a few students struggling to make heads or tails of their sources, as they occasionally ran across scholarly articles in agrarian science or economics journals, and while in times past I would have said "drop it and move on," I suddenly realized that it would be much more compelling reading for me if they talked about what they didn't really understand as opposed to whatever answers they came up with for their more factual questions. This made my little check-ins with them much more interesting as well.

For example, one student wanted to understand more about the FDA [Food and Drug Administration]—what it did, and who was in charge of making decisions. She was a little horrified to find out how many chemicals went into her food and she wanted to know who was in charge of allowing them to be in there. She went to the FDA's website and spent thirty minutes reading and struggling to make sense of it. What she saw was a profusion of faces and names, but no clear answer to the process by which all these preservatives and additives were approved.

She decided to contact them directly, and I convinced her to make a phone call rather than wait for an e-mail to arrive. She spent another ten minutes trying to wade through the automated voice system and get someone on the phone. Even when she raised an actual human, that person ended up not only being unable to respond to her questions (which to be fair, were a little unfocused), but was somewhat insulting to her throughout the entire conversation. I realized that her story of that struggle said more about the FDA than the answers she was looking for.

Another student became obsessed with why we both export and import beef. I'm sure an economist could give a detailed explanation of the mechanics of international trade or discuss economies of scale, but this student just thought it sounded strange not to keep the beef here in the first place.

He set out on a journey of his own to answer this question, with a few inclinations of why this might be the case—that is, the quality of the meat might play a role—and it soon become clear that he had no inkling at all of how the global system of commerce functioned. Nor is it likely that he should, given how little is discussed about it in the places a ninth grader typically goes for knowledge.

I caught him later on the USPS webpage, where he was trying to calculate international shipping rates per pound. In other words, how much does it cost to ship a cow? I asked him what on earth he was doing, and he told me that since no one was able to provide any information about shipping costs, the USPS was the only source he had left. He didn't seem happy about it . . .

It became clear to the teacher that despite the glories of the Internet, it is enormously difficult, in both conception and practice to actually find out the answers to one's questions. So many web sources failed the most basic tests of credibility, while others were poorly curated or impossible to decipher. What slowly replaced the need for content analysis in these research papers was a narrative of what's like to try to use the Internet effectively—that is, a record of the students' thinking process when confronted with challenges.

The aha moment—where I realized what this assignment could actually become, came after a long conversation with a student who was visibly struggling with this project. He ran to my classroom after the day had ended, and at first couldn't speak for a lack of breath. After he calmed down, we had the following conversation . . .

He began with: "Mr. Werberger, I'm thinking of changing my entire investigation," at which point he reeled off a string of non sequiturs that were ostensibly an explanation of this new topic he liked, but I couldn't make sense of them.

"What was your first big question again?" I asked.

"I wanted to find a better alternative to corn," he said.

"Why does the question matter to you?"

"Because I had read in another book that part of the obesity problem in America is from high fructose corn syrup, and because corn is being used for so many products but it's actually bad for the environment to grow so much of it."

"That sounds like a good question. What went wrong?"

"It's too broad, and I know I won't be satisfied by whatever answer I come up with. And it's going to be too hard for a ninth grader to come up with a different crop than the one we have been mostly using since the nineteenth century."

"Okay, so what's the new question?"

"I want to focus more on talking about why and how corn is grown everywhere and how there are actual economic disadvantages to growing so much of it . . . mostly because that is the bulk of what I'm finding on the Internet when I search. I have more sources and it feels more practical to me, so to be honest, I'm more likely to read more about."

I asked him whether he thought the answers to his question or his struggles with his research process would be more useful to the reader. "The research process, I think, because it's more about what happens when you look stuff up, and maybe people could learn from that." At which point he left and announced he was "going to start reading right away!"

The teacher stopped the assignment after just two days of research—some of it fascinating, but some of it incredibly irritating—and asked the students to just start writing their thought narratives. Their goal was to make sense of what they did know, but also to meta-comment—that is, to talk about their process of investigation and what they had learned about the investigation itself. The student who had been challenged by the FDA was instructed to write about that, as was the student curious about shipping rates for cows. In other words, this was a formative and reflective assignment, even though it seemed to be summative.

The students were given some questions to help them write these narratives:

- What prompted them to begin a particular investigation—what was the initial point of interest?
- After each round of research, how was their thinking changing about this topic? Did the topic still matter to them? Did they have the same opinions about it as before?
- Which new questions and new details emerged? Did it confirm or rebut what they thought they knew?
- What was their response to what they were reading?
- Were they aware of how their thinking was evolving? Could they explain how and why their feelings about the topic were shifting?

Jason's Research Blog: CAFOs?

I started out with a very broad question, one that I wasn't entirely sure how to answer or even word properly. I ended up asking, "Is it more profitable sometimes to farm more stuff less efficiently?" This was a flawed question from the get-go for a couple of reasons. One, I was just too vague about "efficiency." Did I mean efficiency in terms of using less energy or resources? Did I mean efficiency in terms of keeping almost every animal at prime quality for slaughter, so that there would be little to no meat failing quality control? Or did efficiency mean minimizing expenses and maximizing income, which would result in my question contradicting itself?

Two, the question was too broad in general. Was I thinking about livestock or crops? Or both? I wasn't sure.

I ran into more trouble when I tried to figure out how I would answer my question. What information did I need? Well, I figured I could try to find some examples of factory farms that are known for cutting corners, find out how much money they're making, then get some examples of more humane farms and do the same. Then I could compare the profits and see who makes more for doing what. This would at least answer a slightly different question: "If you cut lots of corners, will you end up failing as a business or profit greatly, and does the size of your operation matter?"

See, I could do this. I could mask the fact that I don't know what I'm doing with some good writing. Right?

Wrong. Where would I get any of this information? I had no idea, but I did have faith in my trusty friend Google. I tried several fruitless search terms, such as "factory farms," "who owns factory farms," and "factory farm violations." I didn't find much of anything, because all of the farms themselves were nameless! They didn't even have a cheery façade with pictures of happy animals in spacious pastures—they just didn't seem to exist! Given some of the scandals involving factory farms that bubble up into the news every so often, I could see why they would want to keep a low profile.

It definitely seemed like the lack of easily accessible information was by design.

I began to run out of ideas, so I started grasping at straws, looking for whatever information I could get my hands on, so that I could feel like I'd found something. Soon, I was sure I had a lead: a list of undercover investigations by Mercy for Animals. I questioned the validity, not to mention the legality, of hidden-camera investigations without a warrant or anything of the sort.

However, I now knew the names of several companies that owned factory farms! I immediately picked one, Seaboard Foods, and tried to find some information about its income, profits, maybe its infractions, anything. I was hopeful when I found "2013 Annual Report—Seaboard Corporation," but my hopes were quickly dashed.

It turned out that Seaboard Foods is a division of a much larger company with fingers in many different pies, Seaboard Corporation, and this was a report for the company as a whole. Besides that, I just couldn't wrap my head around it. What did all these terms mean? I thought I could just ask Mr. Werberger for help and everything would be fine, but then I caught a cold and had to stay home for several days—one of the most frustrating of setbacks, because you have all sorts of time but you don't feel like doing anything productive. That was basically the end of my progress toward my original goal.

What did I learn from this? For one thing, it's that I can't always find everything I need with Google. In general, it's hard to find information about somebody if you don't know who you're looking for, especially if they just barely have an identity. And that is something that I am now suspicious about: if these are mostly nameless operations, what are they doing that they don't want people to easily find out about. Finally, I also learned my lesson about the importance of knowing better what you want to do in advance, rather than trying to make it up as you go along; if you don't know what you're doing, admit it.

What might I do next? Well, first of all, I should probably get some more realistic expectations. I may have to go out to the supermarket and compare prices, or call some people to figure this out. I will definitely have to look at some different sources; I only wanted information from the farms themselves, so that my claims could not be dismissed as unsubstantiated, but it would probably be a better idea to look for newspaper articles and such about the industry.

It may also be a good idea to change my question. Rather than having to look at lots of hard-to-find information and compare it all, it might be more productive to just see what's going on in general: Are factory farms really so bad? If so, what do they do that's bad? Do their wrongdoings benefit them in terms of the bottom line? And, of course, why should we care?

WORKS CITED

"Undercover Investigations of Factory Farms and Slaughterhouses." MercyForAnimals.org. February 11, 2015. http://www.mercyforanimals.org/investigations.aspx.

"Seaboard Foods-An Integrated Food Company and Home of the Highest Quality Pork Products." Seaboard Foods—An Integrated Food Company and Home of the Highest Quality Pork Products. February 12, 2015. www.seaboardfoods.com/.

Seaboard Corporation. 2013 Annual Report—Seaboard Corporation, 2013. January 29, 2015. www.seaboardcorp.com/wp-content/uploads/downloads/2014/02/AR-12-31-13-Printer-revised.pdf.

"Seaboard Corporation." Seaboard. February 12, 2015. www.seaboardcorp.com/.

Perhaps the educational world is guilty of requiring answers rather than taking the meandering flow of thoughts as evidence of learning itself.

Perhaps there is too much emphasis on creating more things, more physical objects that simply take up space, and not as much emphasis on process. Small moments of brilliance always happen in classrooms, usually during discussions or one-on-one conversations, but which go unrecorded in favor of test scores and essay grades.

As teachers, we all want our students to learn, but the metric for determining this goal has been woefully inadequate—at least for nonarts or nonsports classes. Can a student be considered a mathematician after a high school trigonometry course? Or a practicing scientist after Advanced Chemistry? Yet teachers define mastery as learning some of the basic skills—and a little superficial content—necessary to become a professional, though most of the students never really understand why they are learning it.

And it seems somehow fraudulent to let them graduate high school thinking they are practicing scientists when the current state of scientific understanding in the U.S. belies this very point.

Perhaps a greater mark of the scientist, the historian, or the engineer is not just the ability to focus, but the ability to notice new patterns in old information, and the possibility for new types of information—skills that come from being to think more deeply about what lies right under our noses.

Consider a self-reflection from Neil after his ninth grade class finished a debate on imperialism. The class had been asked to discuss whether patterns from nineteenth-century imperialism were still occurring in the world. After three days of debate preparation, the students argued for forty minutes, and all that was decided in the end was that neither side had a particularly clear idea of what modern-day imperialism might look like. Some of the students were angry and felt their time had been wasted, even after it was pointed out to them that this realization was of greater use than mindlessly arguing a point without any real understanding of it.

Neil took the opportunity to offer a phrase that seems to summarize the point of this book:

Neil 's Debate Debrief: "You don't really know where you are until you're lost"

> I was out hiking in the woods of Becket with a certain Pete when I was twelve. He said those words as soon as I clarified the fact that we had no idea where the heck we were going. He was right. When you're walking the same old hills, driving along the same roads, or cooking in the same kitchen, everything blends together. You really stop paying attention and you don't look at things too hard.
> But when you get lost, when you are taking the road less traveled, or whatever Robert Frost quote you want to shove down my throat, things get different. You look out the window at the new buildings;

you really take a moment to see what is rolling on out there. That is what happened in the Imperialism Debate. I was beautifully lost.

Now, my initial lack of direction wasn't so beautiful and/or poetic. Instead of being all enlightening, being lost was this giant, ulcer-creating beast consisting of frustrated idling in class and sleepless evenings. Then, after a couple days of this, inspiration hit me like a crate filled with 300 of each of the NOFX albums ever made dropped from a C-130. It was just as confusing and painful as it sounds, too.

After this mild epiphany, I realized that I was still totally blind; I had no clue what I was doing. I just had kept on wildly running like an enraged and mildly confused weasel running through a maze. I looked up information that seemed relevant and I then typed words that something in my head was telling me would work. I asked people questions that were probably relevant, and in the end, I had produced something that was wonderful; it was art.

NOTES

1. Jason Stanford, "Mute the Messenger," *Texas Observer*, September 3, 2014, www.texasobserver.org/walter-stroup-standardized-testing-pearson.

2. "SAT, ACT No Longer Required for Admission to 800 U.S. Colleges And Universities," *Huffington Post*, November 28, 2012, last updated April 6, 2015, www.huffingtonpost.com/2012/11/28/sat-act-not-required-colleges_n_2206391.html.

3. "CRWA + Sample Instrument," n.d., http://cae.org/education-professionals/k12-faculty-or-administrator/cwra-sample-instrument.

4. Leo Widrich, "The Science of Storytelling: What Listening to a Story Does to Our Brains," BufferSocial, November 29, 2012, https://blog.bufferapp.com/science-of-story-telling-why-telling-a-story-is-the-most-powerful-way-to-activate-our-brains.

5. David Vaux, "Why I Retracted My Nature Paper: A Guest Post from David Vaux about Correcting the Scientific Record," Retraction Watch, June 19, 2013, http://retractionwatch.com/2013/06/19/why-i-retracted-my-nature-paper-a-guest-post-from-david-vaux-about-correcting-the-scientific-record.

6. Sigmund Freud, "Recommendations to Physicians Practicing Psycho-Analysis," in *The Freud Reader*, ed. Peter Gay (New York: W. W. Norton, 1995), 359.

7. Erik Robelen, "STEAM: Experrts Make Case for Addings Arts to STEM," *Education Week*, December 1, 2011, www.edweek.org/ew/articles/2011/12/01/13steam_ep.h31.html.

8. Elliot W. Eisner, *The Kind of Schools We Need: Personal Essays* (Portsmouth, NH: Heinemann, 1998) p. 56.

9. Shaun McNiff, "Arts Based Research," in *The Handbook of the Arts in Qualitative Research*, eds. J. Gary Knowles and Andrea Cole (Thousand Oaks, CA: SAGE, 2008), 33–34.

10. "This Is Your Brain on Jazz: Researchers Use MRI to Study Spontaneity, Creativity," Johns Hopkins Medicine, February 26, 2008, www.hopkinsmedicine.org/news/media/releases/this_is_your_brain_on_jazz_researchers_use_mri_to_study_spontaneity_creativity.

11. Amanda Rose Martinez, "The Improvisational Brain," *SEED Magazine*, December 14, 2010, seedmagazine.com/content/article/the_improvisational_brain/.

12. "This Is Your Brain on Jazz."

13. Oded M. Kleinmintz, Pavel Goldstein, Naama Mayseless, Donna Abecasis, and Simone G. Shamay-Tsoory, "Expertise in Musical Improvisation and Creativity: The Mediation of Idea Evaluation," *PLoS One* 9, no. 7 (2014): e101568, doi: 10.1371/journal.pone.0101568.

SIX

Making

The craft of making a physical thing, by hand, has slowly disappeared from the American high school curriculum. Schoolwork has become an almost entirely intellectual activity, where even physical tools have become used to test theories rather than to construct an actual object. Tinkering—the art of fooling with something in an attempt to make it better—likewise, has gone missing. These delights have resurfaced in other avenues of a student's life, most notably in Minecraft, wherein students build elaborate game-ified structures online.

Ed Felten's "Freedom to Tinker" movement is taking this one step further in demanding the legal right of technology owners to "break" phones and otherwise creatively manipulate personal devices, which is currently a punishable crime. Beyond questions of ownership, tinkering is a method for not only personal exploration, but for the collective good—the history of technology is after all the history of continuous tinkering.

The treat of the UnHappy Meal project is that it offers a tangible "thing" to make. The students are learning not by reading, but by doing. By making, they encounter the world of the master and the apprentice and resuscitate an older method of education. They must find adults in the field to help them navigate the harder challenges, and discover the pleasures of working with experts who are excited to pass on what they know. The students, in turn, would learn to work with their peers with maturity and purpose, modeling what they have learned from adults.

THE SATISFACTION OF MAKING THINGS BY HAND

One of the premises for this project was that the students would make something physical, something concrete, by hand. This sort of work carries its own intrinsic motivations. Unlike an essay or a lab report, something made by craftsmanship stands on its merits. It works or it doesn't. An audience will judge it as to its quality. A teacher's subjective classroom sense of what an "A" looks like plays very little part in how it's assessed.

The student has a better sense of what success will look like as well, as the product began as a design in the student's mind in the first place. A teacher may direct the student to build a bookcase, but the student has to design the blueprint. And in the end, if it holds books and someone wants to buy it, well, then, who can argue that the student hasn't achieved what they set out to do? If it falls over, then it's back to the drawing board.

There is another, even deeper satisfaction that comes from working with one's hands. In his book *Shop Class as Soulcraft* Matthew Crawford argues that manual work—fixing a car, building a deck, wiring a house—balances the body and the brain in a way the educational system has forsaken, with its rigid delineation between thinking and doing. One has to continually problem solve in order to make something that functions as it should. And one is rewarded by the physical evidence that the problem has been solved.

He writes:

> I began working as an electrician's helper at age fourteen, and started a small electrical contracting business after college, in Santa Barbara. In those years I never ceased to take pleasure in the moment, at the end of a job, when I would flip the switch. "And there was light." It was an experience of agency and competence. The effects of my work were visible for all to see, so my competence was real for others as well; it had a social currency. The well-founded pride of the tradesman is far from the gratuitous "self-esteem" that educators would impart to students, as though by magic. [1]

He compares this to a typical high school classroom, where assignments are so obviously "contrived" and disconnected from any practicality that most students will feel to no real compulsion to complete them beyond toiling for the reward of a grade, which is in and of itself only necessary to move on to the college of one's choice. For Crawford, intellectual work becomes disconnected from the real world, and remains thus abstracted after the student moves through college and into the white-collar world of further abstracted and thus unfulfilling work. And so on.

Contentment comes from, Crawford says, "mak[ing] yourself useful to other people in a straightforward way that engages your own judgment and thinking so that your actions feel like they're genuinely your own." He claims that by eliminating vocational education from the US school system, manual work has become debased—the province of the unlearned—and rendered automatic, machine-like, without thought and creativity. At the same time, white-collar work has become similarly deadened without the application of physical labor or the appearance of useful objects.[2]

DESIGN THINKING

Design thinking is a way to reunite the physical and intellectual sides of learning. The simplest way to describe it? Building workable solutions for real-world challenges. Unlike project-based learning, wherein the problem and the artifact are established by the teacher, the best design thinking projects allow the participants to identify the issues they think need to be addressed. From there, the team identifies the stakeholders whose needs must be taken into account by any solution, ideas are brainstormed, resources gathered, models developed and workshopped, until a final artifact can be presented.

As an example, Emily Pilloton, a co-founder of Studio H, spent a year working with students in Bertie County, North Carolina, an economically depressed rural district with failing schools (only a quarter of the district's ES and MS students were working at state level). The class she and her partner Matthew Miller created met for three hours a day and led students to "conduct ethnographic research in the field, define the community's needs, visualize design that works, and build prototypes in the 4,500 square foot studio." The final project was to design and build a 2,000 square-foot farmer's market to help resuscitate the town.[3]

The students' motivation to finish school rose over the course of the project, and so did their test scores. Studio H has since moved to Berkeley, California, but projects, including the creation of a tiny house, continue. So does its success in sending students, many of whom come from economically disadvantaged neighborhoods, off to college. Project H notes on its website that its female students report having more confidence and more excitement about school, which is particularly meaningful at a time when numerous reports sound the alarm about the low numbers of women going into engineering.

Beyond the matter of confidence, the act of building an object, rather than reading about it, has been shown to increase student comprehension of the material. A Purdue University study from 2009 tested eighth graders' understanding of the human impact on water quality by having half the students build a water purification device and the other half learn from textbooks and lectures. Greater gains in student comprehension happened among the group that built the purifier regardless of students' socio-economic backgrounds or ethnicity. In fact, students struggling with English made the greatest gains of all—as there were no language barriers to trip them up.[4]

Finally, however, this kind of learning has one last application to recommend it. The MET school in Providence Rhode Island and the flagship of the Big Picture Company that is now affiliated with three dozen schools nationally, features "learning through real work" as an essential component of its learning program. Students spend two days a week with a mentor on a real job site, learning the skills of the workplace but also designing projects to be completed at the site and back at the school.

What is the value of working with experts, one on one, outside of the classroom? Mentorship appears to not only offer the chance for a student to gain hands-on experience; it may also provide emotional and psychological support in ways that can benefit students long after the school years are over.

THE IMPORTANCE OF HAVING A GUIDE

Jurgen Klinsmann, the coach of the US Men's National Soccer Team, is also an accomplished baker. He is technically a craftsman, having learned his trade through the German vocational system (*Ausbildungen*). Unlike the United States, but in common with several other European countries, not everyone goes into a liberal arts or engineering college. Rather, students who want to work with their hands—like bakers, but also like carpenters and auto mechanics—become enrolled in guilds and work directly with masters in their field.[5]

Since resuming guild practice in the 1980s, German carpenters who have reached the level of journeyman take to the road—literally. They are required to travel for roughly three years and spend none of their own money on travel or room and board. They look for opportunities to practice their trade and learn new skills. Crucially, during the first stage of the trek, the journeyman is provided with a guide, an older guildsmen who has already made the trip, and can provide some useful advice.[6]

In his 2013 and 2014 State of the Union addresses, President Barack Obama alluded to the successes of the *Ausbildung* system when he proposed the creation of a federally funded vocational training program for high school students. As he put it, "We're working to redesign high schools and partner them with colleges and employers that offer the real-world education and hands-on training that can lead directly to a job and career."

According to the *Huffington Post* article titled "Obama Administration Embraces Career Education," "Some advocates have long argued that vocational education—especially in the model of European schools' apprenticeship system—can help narrow the dropout rate by keeping practically-minded kids interested in classes more tangibly related to their fields of choice." Ostensibly, if students see a practical point for what they are learning, they are more likely to see value in remaining in the school system. [7]

While vocational classes may certainly have an appeal to students who already know they want to practice a trade rather than pursue a college degree, the idea of apprenticeship has another important benefit for students—it provides them a role model and a mentor at a critical stage in their lives.

An article published in *New York Magazine*, "Why You Never Truly Leave High School," sought to explain why people still carry the mental scars from high school trauma deep into their adulthood. Part of the reason is that there are too few adults for every child in our national education system.

Teenagers are placed into a social arena where there are few common denominators between them aside from their ages. Absent contacts from any other age group, they form their own tribal system of values, of language, and of hierarchy—all of which may bear little relation to what is happening in the more diverse world beyond school.

Compounding this problem is that teenagers are beginning to develop the physical infrastructure in their brains to allow them to create complex identities. Their brains are awash in dopamine as the brain reconfigures itself, but until the brain is fully grown, teenagers are at the mercy of the limbic brain, the part that is notorious for stimulating our flight or fight reactions. Because of these chemicals, experiences become more intense, but one could argue fear and insecurity is the most common mental states for kids as they seek to establish status and identity.

The five kids in *The Breakfast Club* (1985)—the jock, the bad kid, the freak, the nerd, and the prom queen—occupy social spaces that still resonate in high school today. Those spaces are regulated by a thousand little humiliations and intimidations whose consequences remain long after these teenagers have become adults. Kids are ashamed by their victimization, and their adult selves can still recall that shame when it happens to their own children in school. In the words of researcher Brené Brown, "High school is *the* metaphor for shame."[8]

The author notes that as adults we go on and replicate this crushing social milieu—that from the school to the workplace to the gym to the Capitol, we live in a "box of strangers" in which we constantly battle our own insecurities in order to build friendships, romance, and status. Whether high schools exist as they do to mirror this reality, or this reality evolves because of our high schools is unclear. But a solution seems self-evident. If teenagers behave this way because they have no adult models, why not give them more adult role models?

THE APPRENTICE AND THE MENTOR

One discipline still keeps the mentor/apprentice model at the core of its practice: the arts. All European art schools require an aspiring student to apply directly to work with a specific artist. While this is less common in the United States, those schools that do operate on this model do so under the theory that the mentor is a master. Students select a master to work with because they want to create art in a similar way.

Moreover, it lends a certain rigor and seriousness to students' studies because they are working with someone who has achieved respect and esteem in the arts community. The mentor knows the student's work better than anyone else, and this creates an intimacy. They understand their student's process and can push them along past the typical obstacles that arise, or help them develop good questions. They are there from conception through execution. The basis of this trust is that the mentor is there from personal investment, not for judgment.

This relationship has the potential to last long after art school and into the professional world. There is a lineage from mentors to mentees in the way they work. What do the mentors gain from this relationship? They have trained students to approach work the same way they do. They create, in effect, a school or a tradition. They are passing the torch, but something of their own work lives on into a new generation. And in turn, the new artists can help the mentor push past their own hurdles. No one makes art alone.

Most American students will not have a relationship like this until graduate school. While there is some continuity in elementary school, where one teacher will often teach every subject and spend the entire day with the same students, children become siloed into different disciplines, with different teachers by middle school, and this continues right through the four years of college. Some undergraduates are snaffled up by professors who want to groom them for their own graduate programs, but this is rare, especially in the liberal arts. Why not establish this kind of opportunity for when the are still kids—when having an adult role model is critical?

MENTORSHIP FOR THE PROJECT-BASED CLASSROOM

So, what does the teacher gain from having students off meeting with mentors rather than sitting in the classroom? The opening of 1,000 doors.

Project-based classes in which the teacher determines the artifact to be maintained are limited by what the teacher can actually do. It is not just a matter of what can be imagined, given the teacher's skill set and knowledge. It is also a matter of knowing how long a given project will take, which resources will be necessary, and how to assist the students throughout the process.

What if those constraints were removed?

What if a history teacher who had no understanding of how to grow vegetables, how to slaughter a cow, how to make cheese or grind flour, or how to make dye from berries, could still ask his students to make a Happy Meal from scratch? What if the teacher assumed that at some point, a farmer, a butcher, a craftsman, and so on, could be persuaded to help his students figure all that out?

Well, if the teacher isn't doing all that himself, then what is he getting paid for?

This is not a flippant question—it is precisely the point of a series of studies conducted by Sugata Mitra, a professor of Educational Technology at Newcastle University. He became famous for what he termed the "Hole in the Wall" experiment—placing computers with Internet connectivity in some of the poorest villages and slums in India. Without enough qualified teachers available to work with these children, Mitra understandably wondered if they could teach themselves.

As an illustration of what he termed Minimally Invasive Education (MIE), computers were embedded into brick walls and adult supervision was removed. He speculated that left to their own devices, and spurred only by their own curiosity, these children would play with the machines long enough, and purposefully enough, to develop some basic computer skills.

Ultimately, the children were assessed by means of a test that was also administered to children who had been given more traditional instruction in computer literacy, and to older students taking a professional IT course.

Mitra writes, "Regarding the learning environment in which all of the three groups accomplish computer literacy, the differences between MIE learning station users and others is significant. The learning method used by MIE learning station users draws upon the expertise of peers, siblings and friends. Each learner is both a learner and a trainer."

His results showed that while the IT students learned quite a bit fairly quickly, all three groups slowly began to equal out over an eight-month period—a period of time in which the MIE students had no adult teachers and no assessments. Mitra concludes, "The unstructured, open and flexible environment of the MIE learning station seems to produce comparable levels of computer literacy amongst learners as compared to formal methods. It does so at a considerably lower cost."[9]

Mitra has since performed other experiments, including giving Italian children textbooks in English to see if they could teach themselves not just biology, but English as well. The success of these children to organize themselves into peer groups, to figure out the resources they needed to learn on equipment that was not terribly familiar for them, has led him to conclude that what students might need from a teacher more than anything is the positive support of a physical presence and unflagging optimism — or what he calls a "Grandmother Cloud."

Assuming a bit more of an active role from a teacher than being grandmotherly, what should a teacher's role be in a classroom where even they might not have the skills or technical knowledge to directly assist a student? If carpentry is the mastery of working with wood, then should teachers be considered masters at understanding how to learn?

One of the experiments at the heart of the UnHappy Meal project was whether the teacher could facilitate the students' work, rather than explaining to them how to do it. After all, it was up to the students to figure out what they needed to know — it would be impossible for the teacher to predict those needs.

Ideally, someone would be found who could help fulfill those needs. If not, then the students would have learned two things — first, how hard it would in fact be to make those items by hand, and two, how to figure out another solution. The teacher would be the model for thinking through the problems of developing questions, determining goals, conceptualizing next steps, and locating the necessary resources. How this worked out in practice is the subject of the next section.

BACK TO THE UNHAPPY MEAL

Organization

The first set of tasks for recreating the Happy Meals had been fairly easily broken down into things animal, vegetable, and, if not mineral, at least it was easier to think of the packaging that way. This meant the top priority was to find someone to help figure out how to procure the meat, someone who could help organize the planting, and someone who could problem solve making paper and ink.

That was oddly easy. The town of New Lebanon, New York has only a few thousand inhabitants, but a substantial number of them are farmers. Even just a few casual conversations in September, long before the students even knew about the project, had turned up a handful of people excited about helping with the various stages of the project.

A visiting artist, Nikki, was interested in experimenting with organic paper and ink, and agreed to mentor the packaging crew. While a number of hunters suggested that a wild deer could be the source of the meat for the hamburger patty (though success in this regard was fairly chancy), local farmers Schuyler and Colby Gail, who raise pigs, among other things, at Climbing Tree Farm became the sponsors of what was termed the Meat and Dairy Crew. Though pig milk was not in the offing, they in turn knew dairy farmers who could help with the cheese component.

The teacher needed a bit of help as well. The very first meeting of the students' project teams in November had revealed a great deal of enthusiasm with not a great deal of direction. While teaching can be likened to project management, the scale, scope, and content of this project made even the first few steps seem daunting. It was difficult to know where to begin, especially as most of the teacher's knowledge about farming was hypothetical.

Fortunately, the Gails knew a homesteader and teacher named Paul who might be able to help. His interest was piqued enough for him to come and visit the classroom and each project team to discuss their goals. As there were five separate teams, the day was grueling but he listened thoughtfully and responded to every question. After a combined hour and a half of troubleshooting, he waited until the students left to deliver the bad news—the kids had great ideas, but no concept of how to start them.

"They need clear, identifiable goals for two weeks for now, for one month from now, for six weeks from now," he said. "And they need them fast. There's no way some of them are going to be successful, either. The weather alone is going to guarantee the tomatoes will fail." He suggested that each team should develop a two week plan with a concrete, realistic goal at the end which could be assessed as a benchmark.

These first benchmarks looked something like this:

> For Team 4, Johann and Isaiah will be the Vegetable team. They will work on getting soil and will develop a schedule to alternate watering between them. For the two week deadline, all the seeds will be planted. Isaiah is also moving on bread, and says it takes two weeks to collect the yeast from the air. His two week deadline—a nice starter colony of yeast.
>
> Tilly has seeds at home for Johann and Isaiah. She will also be in charge of chicken raising, and the cheese. Because of her side interest in the chemicals used for preserving fruit, she is developing an experiment to inject apple slices with calcium ascorbate and seeing what develops. For her two-week deadline, she will conduct and document the apple experiment. She will come up with an action plan for how to make cheese. She will email Paul for more information.
>
> For Team 5, Neil wants actual milk. To procure the milk by hand would be best. The two week plan is reading up on how to acquire milk and how to make cheese.
>
> Frederick and Maria want to make a meatless Happy Meal. They will use cheese and a meat substitute. Their two week plan is to start growing vegetables, and Maria will talk to a local vegan restauranteur about grinding tofu in meal.
>
> BeBe is in charge of toy making and packaging. She plans to make an actual lunchbox. Her two week deadline: to come up with a blueprint/plan for the toy.

The problem of finding time do all this was not actually a concern. The school had a dedicated block of time for hands-on work every Wednesday morning, a blend of community service and weekly chores that saw kids doing everything from chopping wood to working with a local elementary school.

These tasks fit easily within that two and a half hour chunk, and the students were subsequently divided into production teams for Meat and Dairy, Gardening, and what was termed "Organics" for the packaging crew. In other words, four days of the week students would work in their Unhappy Meal teams, but on Wednesdays they'd split into production crews.

Nikki, the artist, agreed to mentor the Organics crew, and while the Gardening crew couldn't actually work in the school garden until spring, they could take advantage of the greenhouse to start their plants. Several faculty members were willing to help out on this end based on their own availability, and to help procure some of the necessary supplies from the various sheds dotting the campus. Colby and Schuyler agreed to advise the Meat and Dairy crew, with the teacher facilitating.

This workaround raised a new challenge, however, which was not immediately clear until Paul's second visit, in time for the first benchmark due date. After what was becoming his traditional rounds of check-ins, he pointed out that the students' communication within the UnHappy Meal teams had been supplanted by the new forms of communication developing among the Wednesday morning work crews, who were all now working more directly together. "When I talked to the students doing the packaging," he said, "they actually didn't know what the rest of the teams were working on that they needed to package!"

The solution was to have each UnHappy Meal team use their weekly check-in time to create project schematics. A good schematic is a map not only of the components of a system, but also details how the pieces go together. In this case, it would require the teammates to remind each other who was working on which piece and what was necessary for each component to be completed. The schematic would become a map of progress for both them and for the teacher, as each student was asked to annotate the drawing with the various steps that had already been accomplished.

The schematic itself was quickly worked into what had become general classroom practice. These maps became the focus of gallery walks, the students critiquing each other's schematics, marking areas that were difficult to understand, praising inventive workarounds, or offering different ideas to challenges. It was graphically clear as well, based on the information in the schematic, who on each team was working and who wasn't (though this was seconded in the student's biweekly updates).

Production

By the third week after the deconstruction, the students and the teacher had created a reasonable way to organize the manual work that would need to go into the Unhappy Meal. Each team had a way of communicating via the schematic the progress they each made as individuals, and the map itself was a useful way to prompt face-to-face conversations during weekly meetings. Each individual student was responsible also for writing an update blog every two weeks to identify challenges met and remaining to be done.

The teams had divided up tasks, with every step labeled and accounted for on the schematic, and the students were then organized by tasks into production crews that meant once a week to carry out their weekly goals. The number of people involved in the project had swelled, as art teachers, farmers, sustainability experts, and science teachers had slowly been pulled in to assist in one task or another.

What would the actual process of production look like? The gardening crew was limited to planting seeds and keeping them warm in the greenhouse until spring (which wouldn't really arrive in April that year due to an unusually cold and snowy winter). When the ground finally thawed, the young plants were transplanted into the garden, but not before the garden itself had to be prepared for the new arrivals.

The Organics crew picked as many of the remaining berries as possible that yet remained so they could experiment with boiling them down to dye. When winter hit in all its glory, they went on to practice paper making from recycled paper, then birch bark, and other alternative substances. Nikki conducted her own experiments for her work, and encouraged the students to try their own ideas and share their results with each other. Over time, breakthroughs happened both by careful research and happy accident, as objects resembling folded paper and ink began to appear in their update blogs.

The Meat and Dairy crew had a more unusual experience. They traveled to Climbing Tree Farm to meet the Gails, who spoke at length about the way constant adaptation and innovation was necessary to keep a farm going. Given that Climbing Tree was a pig farm, what the kids mostly wanted to know about was the butchering process. Schuyler did talk about that at length. At the end she mentioned that she only ate meat that she and her husband had butchered themselves. "That way," she said, "we know the animal had a happy life."

That was the prelude for her bombshell announcement—she offered to help them raise chickens and then slaughter and cook them for the UnHappy Meal project. Tending to the chickens from their arrival in early February through to their slaughter in late April tells a compelling story about adaptation, improvisation, and the importance of expertise and mentorship.

Mr. Werberger's Teacher Journal

> I had known all along that the biggest challenge for this project would be the meat, and I hadn't decided yet how we would handle that. Several hunters in the area had offered to show the kids how to skin and butcher wild game (but as things turned out, no one ended up bagging anything). My initial thought was for them to visit a slaughter-house or just be witness to a butchering and then let them buy meat from the store. One of the students, a militant vegan, had offered to make a grain-based protein patty to substitute for the meat. But none of these options held the allure of actually raising and then killing food.
>
> Being the gentler sort myself, I was surprised at how excited the students got at the thought of harvesting chickens for meat. Several of the kids began bragging about how their families had kept hens when they were younger, or that they had assisted in dressing birds. It's a bit humbling to realize that of all us in the room, I was the one who knew the least about where his food came from.
>
> It was actually easier to order livestock than I thought—one phone call later and I had twenty-five day-old Cornish-Rock Cross chicks on the hook. They arrived February 1st, one day old, and freezing half to death after having been left out on a loading dock for two hours. Amazingly, only one appeared to be dying, and one of the students who wanted to relieve its suffering was shown how to kill it quickly and (hopefully) humanely—an operation that resembles snapping it like whip while holding its head.
>
> That chick was then quickly requisitioned by the biology teacher for a future lab dissections.

Once the chickens had arrived, the students drew up a list of responsibilities and created a schedule to change the litter, water, and food. They created several different makeshift chicken coops as the chicks grew in size. In this, the school's biology teacher, Lily, who had raised chickens before and was willing to house them in her room, assisted them. She saw an opportunity to have a living classroom and potential dissection specimens should things go awry.

She helped the students develop scientific studies. One girl in particular weighed three of the chicks, each of whom she marked with a sharpie for identification, every day to record their growth. In another instance, Lily helped the students diagnose a dying chick with "pasty butt"—essentially, constipation—which tends to be fatal if left untreated. The chick was "quarantined" while everyone waited patiently to see if it could move its bowels. It succeeded and was returned to the makeshift coop and vinegar was added to the water supply to prevent future occurrences.

Eventually, they outgrew both Tupperware containers and the crew had to jerry-rig a coop from two kiddie pools and a huge cardboard box. This increased the amount of time the kids had to spend changing out the bedding and refilling the food and water. Increased space and increased size meant more of a stench, which quickly leached out of the classroom into the entire science building. The chicks also outgrew the scales, which meant the impromptu measuring experiment was curtailed. Thus, the impossibility of keeping them in the room peaked at the same time the kids' interest in taking care of them bottomed out.

There were surprisingly few enclosed places on campus to move them to, considering the school's former history as a working farm. A search undertaken in an old barn revealed an abandoned dovecote. It was a large wire cage on the second floor that looked useful, but which had a large open window that had lost its covering. The ongoing winter—now referred to as the coldest in recent history—meant that subfreezing temperatures and brutal wind would quickly kill the birds unless we could rig up a heat source and close the window.

John, a fellow history teacher who doubled as a carpenter, found a useful alternative on the ground floor—an enclosed room that was close to the power source. Half the students began moving out the chicks while the other half worked with the carpenter and the school librarian, who also raised chickens at home, to transform the room into a chicken coop. It was pointed out that there were a number of worrisome cracks in the walls and floor that offered ingress for predators, so the teacher/carpenter went to work covering the bigger gaps with bits of lumber and pieces of wire fencing.

It took a week for the first casualty to be recorded. It was a mysterious death. The chicken's crop had hardened and there were no other discernible signs of injury. The biology teacher performed an autopsy and discovered the crop was filled with blood, which accounted for its hardness. The kids speculated the chickens had pulled down a heat lamp and the metal table it was fastened to and the dead chick had been crushed.

The next death was more obvious—the chicken was missing a head and there was no blood around the body. One of the facilities staff said it was a weasel, which was horrible news, since weasels could slip through the tiniest cracks in the walls or the floor.

"Yep, you'll probably lose all of them unless you can trap it, though it's technically against the law to do that in New York," he said. "It's not hunting season."

The end result was three more dead chickens in two nights—one with a fractured skull, again caused by a falling lamp, which the kids speculated was caused by a rumpus of chickens fleeing the weasels, and two more found without heads and crammed into a far corner of the coop. The more intact chicken was requisitioned for an on-the-spot dissection attended to by the entire freshman class.

The chicken was quickly whittled down and its various components pulled out and marveled at. The teacher suggested that the kids should create a chicken schematic, similar to their UnHappy Meal maps. No sooner said than done. One of the students who had a bit more experience with farming than the others pointed out how many of less edible parts—the cloaca, feathers, feet, and gizzard—were in fact incorporated into chicken nuggets. Apparently, he knew farmers that sold these bits to the factories.

Ultimately, however, this sudden and rapid depletion in the flock meant that the chickens would have to be moved to a more secure location—in this case, to Climbing Tree Farm, which had a more secure coop. Though they would lose contact with the chicks for the last two weeks prior to rendering, the students had been learning quite about improvisation and adaptation, as well as crushing loss. They had also worked with several different adults, each of whom had different skills and knowledge to impart, and had gotten used to having any number of drop-ins as the project raised curiosity around campus.

Reconstruction

The remaining question was how these meals would be assembled and if the harvesting would go as planned. The students approached the two chefs who ran the dining hall and asked for help. As it turned out, Chef Rebecca Joyner was affiliated with the Hudson Valley's Chefs' Consortium, an organization of New York chefs working to promote farm-to-table cooking. She and her associate Chef Josh Coletto, saw an opportunity to not just teach the ninth graders how to cook, but how to make a statement with their food.

In her mind, the meat from the chickens could feed the entire school, and she and Chef Josh quickly envisioned a menu consisting of chicken burgers, pots of farm cheese, handmade bread and condiments, and root cellar fries. Thus, the last Hands to Work, Wednesday, May 14, would feature a community meal, prepared by the students, with their assembled UnHappy Meals front and center. The meal would thus become a sort of exhibit, and a coming together around the idea of food. Eating would become a sort of participatory performance that the students could direct to their own ends.

She and Chef Josh met with the students once a week, and drew up a schedule that dictated when the students would come to the kitchen to make the various components over the five days prior to the luncheon. The key question was, of course, how and when would the chickens be rendered?

The challenge was two-fold: (1) find someone who could do it, and (2) find a place to do it at. In the end, in order to be able to serve the chickens to the school, the killing had to be done in a USDA certified facility (a mobile "meatwagon") and the person doing the killing had to be okay with a dozen freshmen horning in on the experience.

Mr. Werberger's Teacher Journal

Our chefs had found a young chicken-dispatcher in the area who was not only happy to drive his mobile killing wagon out to us, but also to teach the kids how to do the job—or who at least wasn't scared at the thought of working with the students.

The first step was setting up the equipment and getting the heat going in the scalding tub. Meanwhile, several students split off to drive out to the farm and round the chickens up into cages. When I had last visited them, I found out they hadn't actually free-ranged much, despite having been put into an enclosure outside once the weather warmed up. The farmer tending them explained they had gotten so used to being restricted indoors they didn't know they could move around and explore, so they had worn out a patch of ground only as big around as their shed. They could barely support their weight and waddled, almost painfully, as they walked.

But this time, as we approached, they seemed healthier and more curious. In fact, a dozen of them clustered around my feet as their fellows were hauled up one by one and placed into the transporter cages. I knew they only assumed I was bringing feed, but I admit I felt a slight maternal instinct, and no small amount of guilt for what was about to happen.

When we arrived back at school with the chickens, we found we had a larger audience waiting for us. Several of the other Hands to Work teams had gathered, along with many of the adults, and our chicken "processor" was explaining each of the killing and cleaning stations to them—from the Cones of Death to the scalder, plucker, and cleaning table, and all the hoses and buckets and runnels festooning the equipment.

There wasn't much ceremony to it. He grabbed four chickens at a time, stunned them slightly, and placed them upside down in each cone with just the head sticking out the bottom. He ran his knife through the chicken's neck and sliced outward, severing the carotid. The dying chickens kicked for a bit (one of the students timed the length of the process) and squirted feces into the air with their exertions. The blood poured into the runnels and down into a bucket.

After they had bled out, they were removed and put to the side and another four selected and dispatched. This process recurred four more times. The waiting chickens didn't seem to be aware of what was happening and some were cradled by the students, who thoughtfully turned their heads away as the killing was happening. The students did not actually kill them—they weren't really legally allowed to—but instead they helped with the next process.

One by one the chickens were briefly scalded to loosen the feathers and then placed in a tumbler lined with rubber finger-like projections. This spun like a clothes dryer and neatly removed nearly all the feathers in a short amount of time as the chickens caromed off the sides. Any remaining feathers were plucked out by hand and the naked birds placed in a barrel of ice water.

The final step was to remove the feet and heads and clean out the innards. The students handled this part—with more alacrity than I thought they would, but with an appropriate solemnity. Over the next two days the students returned in small batches to the kitchen where they deboned the chickens and separated the usable meat from the stock stuff.

Yes, it was a harrowing experience. I was emotionally exhausted for much of the day, even though I hadn't wielded a knife at any time. But I had spent more time with these chickens than anyone else, had worried over them, had gone out in the middle of the night when the students missed a feeding, had spent days trying to solve the weasel problem . . . and it was my fault they were being killed. On the other hand, that's what they were for, right?

We were able to see the results of our work once the chickens had been dissected. Some had arteriosclerotic hearts—the effects of morbid obesity! On the other hand, the meat was huge and healthy looking—the slaughterer couldn't get over it, and he complimented the kids several times over. The students felt the chickens had had a good life, at least, even if it had ended violently and so soon. I was left wondering if the meat will have a sort of aura about it—some way to "taste the difference," and I was curious to see how they would educate their peers as to the nature of what they would eat.

While the teacher had felt comfortable teaching the intellectual side of the project, the hands-on component had been a mystery from the beginning. How does one teach a skill that one doesn't know? The answer had been to involve as many people from the community as possible. The students would learn the practical means to make the UnHappy Meal from these experts, but they would also watch how adults collaborated and problem solved in the real world.

The rhythms and rewards of work beyond school are different. Activities are not generally divided into small chunks of time and answers are not obvious. If it is difficult to approximate this reality in the classroom, then perhaps the answer is to get the kids out of the classroom. Enable them to develop adult relationships based on mutual respect rather than social hierarchy.

What was the impact of this on the students? How did they feel about these weekly interludes of manual labor, or working with farmers, artists, craftsmen, and teachers?

Selections from Natalya's Update Blogs

February

For a while, I thought that we wouldn't actually buy chickens, and just go to a local farm and buy meat from there. I didn't know how easy it was to get chickens. The idea of growing and caring for these chickens seemed kind of crazy. Three teenagers with other things happening in their day, such as sports and theater, caring after chickens? My mom always complains about how I could barely take care of my dog, let alone after twenty-five chickens! Would our teachers and peers be able to trust us with this big responsibility?

I have never worked with livestock, and wasn't experienced at all. I had to learn quickly, because the next day is when I would have to start taking care of them daily. They need to be frequently checked on! They poop A LOT, and tend to drink all of their water rather quickly. We provide them with 24/7 access to food, so that they can grow and develop into meaty chickens . . .

My group had decided that we would check on them three times a day, at every mealtime. Breakfast, lunch, and dinner. The missing factor in the cleaning was, who was going to do it. We all discussed what times would be best for each individual. I volunteered to make a schedule on Google drive that we would all have access to.

Taking care of these chicks have sure been a great adventure. It takes a lot of time out of your day, but it doesn't bother me. I get to spend lots of time with little living, breathing things. I remember that I once stayed with them for over three hours with Josie—obsessed much?

Tracking their growth has also been fun. It's cool to see how fast they grow, and have evidence of that. The thing I'm most proud of so far is that none of them have died under our care (yet!). There is still a lot of time left to learn from them, and track them before they are slaughtered in April.

March

As the chickens were growing and getting bigger, they started to need more attention and things needed to change so that it could fit their needs. First off—they were getting way too big for the little buckets/ bins we put them in. The poop was starting to become inches of smelly, nasty "bedding." So, on a hands to work day, we moved them into two separate kiddie pools. It took little effort, since there were three of us.

At first, we couldn't decide where to put them. The idea of putting them outside was quickly eliminated because they still needed the heat lamps and the temperature a specific amount. I looked up that for each week they grow, the temperature should decrease by five degrees. For this, I tried to raise the heat lamp a little bit every once in a while. They stayed in those kiddie pools for a short amount of time until they grew even more and needed to be moved again!

After that, we went over to Schuyler's farm to help out with some tasks. We helped them shovel out snow in different places throughout the forest. We needed to do this to have a separate pen for the mama pigs with their babies. Sometimes, the other pigs can squish the piglets accidently. Separating them makes it less of a risk. We got to spend time with the pigs, and it was really fun. The two-hour work was tough, being in the cold and working our muscles, but it was worth seeing the little piglet that I got to hold.

During the two hours of shoveling, I learned some pretty interesting stuff from Schuyler and Colby. For example, I didn't know that farming as a job has such a low income. I thought that you would earn a lot of money, because meat that is well-grown costs more! In my experience, buying locally is much more expensive than buying meat from a supermarket that got it from 1,000 miles away. It's a clear representation of how f-ed up the meat industry is.

This job takes so much work. I can't imagine being a farmer. Colby works about twelve to sixteen hours a day! I truly admire Schuyler and Colby though. They take up so much time and money raising and caring for these animals (the good way), and it seems as if they do it for a good cause. Sometimes I wish we could help them more, because I know Colby would love the help.

April

Back to the chickens being in the barn. They are doing okay—although sometimes I think that they weren't ready for the cold weather. We moved them because they were getting too big, and didn't have enough room anywhere on campus. I don't think they are ready because they seem really cold. They are always huddled in big clumps. I'm just glad that we placed some heat lamps in there. I also noticed that they would go through their water and food really fast. They seemed really hungry and thirsty every time I would refill their food and water—like literally fighting each other for some room in the food bin or water tray.

Another problem with having the chickens in the barn is predators!!! About three chickens have died already from weasels, or some other chicken eating animal. It was between the weasels or some kind of wild cat. Two of the chickens were decapitated! Their heads were completely gone! At first I didn't know if I was fascinated, or confused. It was really cool to see how an animal could completely take the head off of them. It also makes me wonder why it didn't eat the rest of the chicken, it just left it there. The head is an odd spot to eat from. I would think that it would go for the meaty part of the chicken.

The other chicken died from an accident. I think it was our fault :(On a Thursday night, I was casually walking up to the barn to do my duties. When I got there, I noticed that a chicken was acting completely different from the others. It was under the wood, looking like it was stuck or something. I noticed that the big metal object (that held the heat lamps) was knocked over, and right next to this chicken. I put it back on the carton, and took the chicken out to examine it. It appeared to me as if it were dying. Its eyes were really swollen, and it couldn't get up to walk. It also seemed as if it had trouble breathing.

I called [Lily] over, and asked her for her opinion. She too, thought that it was dying. We put it back in the coop right under the heat lamp. We were to check on it again tomorrow. Just as I was leaving, I noticed that the heat lamp's wire was too low, to the point that the chickens could walk on it and sit on it. I then put two and two together and gave the chicken a C.O.D. (cause of death). His or her death was due to the metal object falling on it, because the chickens knocked it over when it was too low.

May

Well, we finally did it! The journey of the chickens has finally ended. This past Wednesday for Hands to Work, we slaughtered them and defeathered them, and cut them into the kind of chicken you see at the supermarket. It was kind of a long process. First, Keith had to put the chickens into this cone, so that there was some control when he was cutting their necks. After he cut them, he let their blood drain out into the bucket that was placed under the cones. From this step, I learned that the chickens continue to move even after you have cut through their throat.

It was kind of scary, because they were just moving and twitching uncontrollably, while bleeding out. I think that this was the most challenging part of the process, because it made you think if the chickens were suffering, and how they must feel. I timed how long it took some chickens to completely stop moving after being cut. The average was one minute and fifty-five seconds . . .

We also had to cut out and separate the heart, neck, liver and feet. We had to place them in bags, because these parts of the chickens could be used for something else. They were to be taken out, and be used for another purpose other than our happy meals . . .

After gutting out the chickens and getting rid of what we don't need, we packed everything and our day was over. The next day for F Block, we went over to the kitchen to Josh, the chef. He was teaching us how to correctly cut up a chicken into pieces. It was pretty interesting, because there are specific techniques that you need to use. Now whenever I need to cut up a chicken by myself, I don't have to look on Google.

I learned some rather interesting things from this experience. We raised our chickens, with far more time than what the big companies allow. The companies that raise hundreds of chickens, only let them live to about six weeks. We let our chickens grow to about nine to ten weeks. This was a big difference, because we had way more meat than we expected.

After the slaughtering, I talked to Rebecca Joyner. I had asked her if how much meat we had was enough to feed the whole campus. She got excited, and told me we had more than enough. She was expecting about sixty pounds from what we raised, and actually got around eighty. This means that each of the chickens were around six to seven pounds, compared to a supermarkets chicken of three to four pounds. It was exciting for us to be able to do these kind of things, and am really glad I had the opportunity.

The "chicken tenders" had had the most visceral experience of all the work teams. Yet all of the production crews had learned responsibility and improvisational thinking. What had they been doing when they were not in their work teams, or meeting over UnHappy Meal schematics? Working on the intellectual side of this project—making not food, but art from chickens, cheese, and recycled cow manure.

NOTES

1. Matthew Crawford, "Shop Class as Soulcraft," *New Atlantis* (Summer 2006): 7–24, www.thenewatlantis.com/publications/shop-class-as-soulcraft.
2. "'Soulcraft' Honors an Honest Day's Work," NPR, July 12, 2009, www.npr.org/templates/transcript/transcript.php?storyId=106513632.
3. Tina Barseghian, "Design Thinking Sparks Learning in Rural N. Carolina," Mind/Shift, November 9, 2010, ww2.kqed.org/mindshift/2010/11/09/design-thinking-sparks-learning-in-rural-n-carolina/.
4. Kim Medaris, "Study: Hands-On Projects May Be Best Way to Teach Engineering and Technology Concepts," Purdue University News, January 28, 2009, news.uns.purdue.edu/x/2009a/090128DarkStudy.html.
5. Brian Blickenstaff, "Where Jurgen Klinsmann Comes From," *Deadspin,* May 27, 2014, screamer.deadspin.com/where-jurgen-klinsmann-comes-from-1582195767).
6. Klaus Grimberg, "He Who Travels, Dispels Prejudice," *Atlantic Times,* June 2008, www.atlantic-times.com/archive_detail.php?recordID=1353.
7. Joy Resmovits, "Obama Administration Embraces Career Education," Huffington Post, November 13, 2013, www.huffingtonpost.com/2013/11/13/obama-career-education_n_4262860.html.
8. Jennifer Senior, "Why You Never Truly Leave High School," *New York Magazine,* January 20, 2013, nymag.com/news/features/high-school-2013-1/index2.html.
9. Mitra Sugata et al., "Acquisition of Computing Literacy on Shared Public Computers: Children and the 'Hole in the Wall,'" *Australasian Journal of Educational Technology* 21, no. 3 (2005): 407–426, www.ascilite.org.au/ajet/ajet21/mitra.html.

SEVEN

Bridging Body, Mind, and Soul

There was much more to the project than discovering how a seed or a chick eventually wends its way to the plate. This was ultimately about art.

Matt Crawford's *Shop Class as Soulcraft* argues that linking thought and handwork balances the brain. The UnHappy Meal was an experiment to bring in a third level of engagement—soul—to transform the act of making into an even more holistic enterprise. The hypothesis was that artistic thinking would create a deeper student investment in the UnHappy Meal project by allowing them to find not just new ways to express themselves, but a greater purpose for the artifacts they would create.

The students made three separate mental breakthroughs over the course of the project that justified this experiment:

1. The students each developed a personal poetic "language" to express complex ideas through simple art projects—that is, they began to understand how to use artifacts as metaphor and synecdoche.
2. They learned to communicate their ethical and political concerns through these artifacts.
3. They established their own goals for personal growth through the project, and learn to assess their performance to the standards they wanted.

Beyond that, however, they had not yet made anything that could be considered "art," unless research itself could be considered an art form.

A MODEL FOR ARTS-BASED RESEARCH

Arts-based research, as defined by Elliot Eisner and Shaun McNiff, is an investigative methodology that emphasizes a sort of play on the part of the researcher. The effect of the observer is not minimized—it is embraced as a resource that can deepen understanding, as can any interactions with an audience. Answers are less important than interactions, as it can be argued that anything that narrows the researcher's focus could result in the loss of unexpected insights from pursuing odd leads.

Janinka Greenwood describes an arts-based research project in New Zealand. A group of nonnative speaking Maori teachers in an immersion program to learn the Maori language attempted to use dramatic theater to explore indigenous culture and potentially use traditional stories to highlight contemporary issues. The participants were asked, however, to explore their own reactions to the dichotomies and similarities of Maori and Western performances, and to be aware that they were consciously reshaping the stories according to their own beliefs and desires.

Finally, they were instructed to think of the audience—to imagine how the perspectives of the viewers might change the meaning and intent of the performance. To that purpose, frequent collaboration and debriefing between the researchers was critical, as these discussions provided a window into the audience's perceptions. Thus, multiple readings of these legends were possible, and each reading opened up a window into the values of those hearing or telling the story. In essence, the participants came to know not just the Maori language, but also themselves and their colleagues better.

The results, Greenwood writes,

> were that the participants reported acquisition of new skills, and also tracked their own individual evolving understandings of complex issues of postcoloniality, biculturalism, ecology, and Maori self-determination, anchoring these in dramatic symbols, role and text. As a group we found significant parallels between our art-based approach and participatory action research . . .
>
> The fusion of research and consequent action that is a feature of action research was also a strong element in our approach as was successive layering of data collection, analysis and sharing of tentative understandings.[1]

A simpler way of explaining this might be to say that the participants were guided through an ostensibly academic investigation by making themselves part of the program of study. Rather than remaining apart from their subjects and acting as silent recorders, they became performers. What they learned become more broadly applicable to their lives.

This was possible because each of the participants was, as Greenwood notes, both practiced in research and in dramatic theater. The ninth graders undertaking the UnHappy Project did not start out with either advantage. At the beginning of school they had begun developing the critical eye of investigators—looking critically at details, developing questions, searching for credible resources, and writing their conclusions—to meet one deficiency. What was missing was art itself.

FIRST ATTEMPTS WITH ART

Art is a way of seeing the world and communicating about it. It is multimodal and all five senses can be utilized. Yet art is also metaphorical—an artifact says more than the sum of its parts. Therefore, it relies heavily on poetics rather than literality to make its point. Literal art is generally bad art. Clever art can twist the banal to create new perspectives and insights for the audience by making new associations and linkages in the beholder's mind. A chicken burger is therefore not just a chicken burger—it's a statement.

A short period of time after the first deconstruction of the Happy Meals had taken place, the teacher realized that the artistic process had not been broached explicitly in the classroom by having the kids simply make a piece of art. Something that touched on creativity, adaptability, and self-expression, all important components of my scope and sequence for ninth-grade history. The students had just completed a long assignment on the Age of Imperialism—perhaps the students could respond personally and artistically to what had been some horrifying reading material.

The challenge was that the kids could not create something obvious to explain the events of the past—as in, an image of a white man striking a Congolese porter. The goal, instead, was to mimic the creative process of an artist. Beverly Naidus had described her efforts to get her art students to connect empathically and emotionally to pervasive social issues. In the same way, the students would be asked to connect personally to imperialism's assumptions and consequences and create an object that expressed that connection.

The only question: How does one teach that?

This challenge was posed to the chair of the Arts Department at Darrow. How could one develop an arts lesson for a history class that wasn't a simple add-on to an existing project—as in, build a papier mâché replica of the Great Pyramids—but rather could serve as the foundation for a new curriculum that placed artistic thinking first? The chair invited the teacher to the next department meeting for a full discussion.

Mr. Werberger's Teacher Journal

> I presented my question to them and then stepped out of the conversa-
> tion to let them talk to each other about how they might solve the
> problem. No concrete plans emerged from the discussion, but the ques-
> tions they asked each other were important and did help me under-
> stand how artists begin to conceptualize their own projects.
>
> The big question that my proposal raised consumed the bulk of the
> meeting time: What is the point of art? Is it to provoke a response in the
> audience or express something the artist cannot say by conventional
> means? Does it clarify or confuse? Is there an end point—a product—or
> is it just an endless process. Can art depict anything? An emotion? A
> concept? A visceral feeling? A response?
>
> These questions were interesting to me because they are precisely the
> sorts of questions that are not asked in the academic core classes. I can
> truthfully say that I have never been part of a history department meet-
> ing—no matter how brilliant the faculty—that began with an honest
> attempt to clarify what "history" was, or what it meant to "do it."

"Why am I doing this?" is the primary question behind any worthwhile
intellectual activity. It is also ostensibly the key to Understanding by
Design, PBL, or any student-centered educational technique. Yet teachers
are required to look at the Common Core or other state and federal standards for the answer to that question. It is as though any deeper investigation into what science or mathematics are, into literature or history, are
considered either irrelevant or understood so completely that there is no
point in asking. But the kids ask this all the time, don't they?

Historians clearly do not spend their time answering true/false and fill
in the blank questions, nor do they write essays. What do they do, then?
In 1985, William H. McNeill, then acting president of the American Historians Association, said that historians " carefully and critically" create our
"collective memory." But he also claimed that understanding how perspectives on the past are continuously changing is the only way to grasp
"the confusing flow of events that constitutes the actual, adult world." In
other words, facts are less relevant than understanding how one comes to
decide which facts are legitimate and useful.[2]

Instead of fetishizing their discipline's core beliefs and imagining students would understand them via some process like osmosis, these artist-
teachers actively wrestled with their founding beliefs about art itself before setting their students to tasks.

On a more practical level, they also wondered if the students would
even understand the point of the activity, if what was being proposed
was too abstract. Did making the project explicitly be about imperialism
make it too challenging, or too limited, or was this the only way to guarantee the kids some concrete, graspable way in?

Apart from that, did the students have the tools to be successful? They had to gauge whether the students had any experience with what was essentially conceptual political art. Were there models, current artists working in the genre work they could examine? They had to know what was possible in order to make their own work.

It was agreed that the students should begin by looking at artists who worked explicitly with the themes of oppression and control—to see how these artists used their work to reveal the way domination, racial or political, intruded into their own lives. Perhaps the students could be prodded to look at how they experienced their own micro-aggressions based on power dynamics in their day-to-day lives.

How often were students allowed to make their own decisions about how they spent their time during the school day despite the assurances they were learning how to be adults? How often do people in positions of authority assume automatically that they know what is better for the kids than the kids do? Don't students' peer relationships reinforce some of those very same inequalities of status they experienced at the hands of adults?

Could the students make the leap from their own experiences to those of the people of the Congo or British East Africa that they had studied during the previous unit, and make a piece of art that bridged the centuries for the audience?

Mr. Werberger's Teacher Journal

> Before anyone makes the obvious objection to this discussion, yes—I should have begun this process right at the beginning of imperialism investigation in the first place. The first time a lesson is taught, it's much easier to see the mistakes by looking back. Fortunately, I believe teachers can learn from failure just as do students.

As the discussion continued, the artists listed the daily activities that had to be reinforced—the use of writing prompts to stimulate thinking, the stages of experimentation and making, the role of group discussion and reflection to meditate on the process of creation. The last question concerned the materials. Was it best for the students to make something by hand or create something more performance-based? Where would they work? What sorts of material could they use?

One idea, ultimately discarded, was to force the students to forage for their supplies—to treat them like the colonized peoples who had to scramble to survive. To say, "Use what's around you. You can't have art supplies. Go dig in the dumpster." It would, theoretically, unleash their frustration and rage. In the larger picture, it would teach them something about art—that it doesn't have to be something you get supplies for. You have to dig for yourself and adapt.

Another idea, also discarded, was to have them use some ubiquitous material as a way to link every individual artifact together for the whole class but still allow for each individual to express him or herself uniquely. Even better, a toxic ubiquitous material. Have the form match the function; if discussing ethical toxicity, why not use a poisonous resource.

In the end, constrained by time and space, two faculty members volunteered to host a few mini-classes for the students and to work in collage or clay. The students were instructed to meet in the art classrooms for a week, with an intentionally vague disclaimer that they would learn a new way to express themselves apart from writing essays and blog posts. For the teacher, this was an opportunity to see if there was a correlation between history and arts pedagogies.

In each case, the class started by exposing the students to existing models of work. They watched short interviews with Kara Walker, who explained the origins and meaning of her *Gone with the Wind*-inspired silhouettes, and Ai Weiwei (the focus in this case was on his "Sunflower Seeds"). The students were then asked to write a brief response to the videos and discuss the meanings they found in the artists' work and whether they thought the artists were "successful." In other words, did the form perform the function the artists intended?

The next day's task was making. The students were asked to choose one of three words—either "power," "voice," or "limitation" and were then challenged to capture that word in clay. There were no requirements, rubrics, or grades. The only goal was for people to understand their artifact. They had ten minutes to perform this task.

As with most projects, the students had different levels of success in self-starting. In this case, however, the challenge seemed to be harder for the kids who were normally diligent, the ones who knew how to be successful in class by following all the correct steps. They were unsure of what do with their lump of clay, and one student essentially boycotted the proceedings by making a cartoon-like snake with comical pop-eyes and announced that it meant nothing at all. Some of the students, however, immediately began creating small sculptures as though they had a finalized piece already clear in their minds.

At the end of the ten minute construction, each student was asked to deliver a brief explanation of the work and the message. The audience was asked to reflect back on the work, using the same formula as before: Was the work successful in delivering the artist's intent? The students were good about talking thoughtfully about even the least fortunate results and tried to honor each student's attempt. Some of the students admitted their work wasn't well planned or executed, but they were able to articulate why that had happened and what they might do differently next time. These first constructions were then tossed back in the bin.

For the third day, the students were given an entire period to create a new artifact, this time in collage. Again, no specific requirements were given. When the students asked for help, they were asked questions instead: "What are you trying to say? Do you see any materials that might help you say that?" Occasionally, they would receive a hint to alter these resources in some way—to add paint to the images they had chosen, or if using cardboard, to distress it by stripping away layers—but there was very little direct instruction. The idea was simply to play with possibilities.

Before the grand unveiling and critique for the fourth day, the students were asked to write a brief self-assessment or reflection on their blogs. The prompt was: What is your message, and why did you choose the materials you did? This was essentially a rough draft of an artist's statement. Cady, who had created a collage of a flower growing through a brick wall while another died behind it from construction paper, wrote:

> I created a work that depicts the struggle of overcoming limitations. I chose the word limitation to work with because I think World Civilizations is a class that has many limitations in some aspects and completely free reign in others. . . . I used cardboard and construction paper to make this piece because I felt I would have more control over how it looked and what it represented as opposed to using cutouts from a magazine. When people see this I want them to think about why limitations exist. Is it for us to be humbled like the dying flower, or encouraged like the healthy flower?

For the critique, the artifacts were assembled around the room and each student was given a piece of paper and something to write with. They were instructed to sit in front of their piece, and write responses to the following three questions:

- What strikes you most about the work (in this case, "the form")?
- What is the piece trying to say (in other words, "the content")?
- Is the work successful?

They were given two minutes to write, then everyone was asked to move one artifact to the left with their paper and then write down their answers to the very same questions. This went on until every piece of art was critiqued by every member of the class. Again, the more literally minded students struggled to make sense of what was in some cases conceptual work. One student, sitting in front of a pyramid of cardboard chunks, gave up in frustration. He was told to just relax and think about it for a minute. He said, "I *am* thinking. I'm thinking about Teddy Roosevelt."

In some respects, the process bore similarities to the habits of mind the students had been cultivating in the history classroom. Thinking routines like the See, Think, Wonder exercise; the performance of critical rounds; and self-reflection were all common tools by this point. This difference was the reliance on empathy to extract meaning from the artifacts, and the confusion that had been caused by the insistence that was seen was less important than what was intuited.

While the students did not seem enthusiastic about keeping their creations, they did have some interesting responses when prompted by two reflection questions: What is the difference between artistic expression and historical writing, and is it a useful way to think?

Example 1:

"I have brought more depth to my thinking patterns. I'm thinking outside the box. And I'm expressing it in other ways than the written word. I have used ways of art to express the pain that the natives went through. I have used drawing to show the metaphorical representation of the difference between the Belgians' way of [conquest] and the British way of [conquest]."

Example 2:

"When I started working on my artwork in [Nikki's] room, I didn't have much to start with. Some of the few materials to use were cardboard, paper, magazines, and things to color with. I immediately started thinking about how I could put all these things together. I then took too much time with the thinking process, and she told me that I didn't have to put too much effort and time for my work to be creative. I then thought about this, and realized that what she told me would work. I ended up creating something out of cardboard, and it expressed what I aimed for: power."

Example 3:

"Creative thinking as you get older dissipates. Does it really or do we just cover it up, like smothering a flame? I think every adolescent realizes that they have lost creativity when they try to sit down and draw and have to spend time thinking of what to draw. . . . I have since age five been struggling to hold on to my piece of mind, but still let things flow. . . . I believe we are getting to the point where we can spit out formulas and theorems—not actual thought that we created, but just something we memorized. We have created boundaries around everything. So how can we change?

"Amazingly art which doesn't say anything out loud sometimes speaks louder than our voices ever could. We have all experienced being unheard, feeling alone. So to be heard we need something to show it maybe that canvas is your voice in a poem, or a wall of graffiti, whatever it is it's a call to be heard. So in class we have dredged up a memory of that feeling and created a booklet expressing that feeling how we feel it. It's different for everyone. There is no correct or incorrect. Just understanding.

"History is the poet, the man with the spray can, he is writing what he sees through his eyes. Therefore, history is an opinion with no right or wrong."

MAKING ART WITH MEANING

By February, the ninth graders had practiced nearly every skill that seemed essential to becoming working artists.

- They had learned to see details as springboards for questions, and not to overlook the obvious.
- They had practiced giving critique, and had become adept at responding to the feedback they received.
- They had conducted several research assignments and had learned to query themselves during the investigation phase—to constantly reassess what they were searching for, and why, and how this information was changing their purposes.
- They had found adults in the community they could work with to supplement what their teacher didn't know or didn't have time to help with.
- They had embarked on at least one session of art making and had used that opportunity to reflect on how different forms of self-expression give rise to new forms of knowledge.
- They had learned investigation skills—they had examined where their current things were made and where trash went when they threw it away, they had studied imperialism in the nineteenth century, they had analyzed primary sources and written essays.
- They had dismantled one of the most symbolic forms of mass consumption and begun to carry out their own unique investigations from the parts.

Moving forward, the danger was that they would become concerned with remaking the Happy Meals exactly as they had found them during Deconstruction Day. The point of the exercise was not to make a clone of the meal, but to make something new—something that embodied the idea of sustainability and something that could function as a palette for the students to express themselves. The short experience the students had had with the art teachers was meant to address that, but it had not likely become a habit of mind yet for them to think metaphorically.

Another danger of course, as Paul had mentioned during his first check-in with the UnHappy Meal teams, was that it was unlikely they would be able to collect all the ingredients, much less combine them together in some way resembling edible food. The vegetable might not be able to get their crops in the ground, and the Organics team had a very small window within which to collect ripe berries in the spring and figure out a workable ink from them.

Mr. Werberger's Teacher Journal

In my first few years as a project-based teacher, I had struggled to create projects that the students could be successful with. I found myself changing the parameters of project halfway so that the students could at least produce something by the end. The projects that failed left everyone with a bad taste in their mouths, and a feeling that a lot of effort had been wasted. My mantra, which I borrowed from my former co-teacher Mark, became "Complex problems yield simple solutions, simple problem yield complex solutions."

The teaching project that I led this year with—asking students to produce a short how-to video during the first week of classes—was a simple project that had been successful at meeting its key goals. However, I had transgressed that mantra with the UnHappy Meal project, and I had done so purposefully. The idea was deceptively simple—just make some food. But the execution was devilishly difficult, especially given the handicaps of seasonal changes, daily schedules, vacations, usable space, and so on. I honestly didn't know if we could actually pull this off, and I had been clear about that with the principal from the very first day.

Given that all went well with the chickens, there would be enough food for everyone to eat a chicken burger, and I had confidence everything else—milk for the cheese, grain for the bread, turnips for the fries—would come our way, thanks to the chefs. That was actually out of my hands, for the most part. No, it was the UnHappy Meals—the component that was supposed to reflect the singular vision of each of the students—that was in question. Was there a way to reconceptualize our likely failure as success?

In his Toaster Project, Thomas Thwaites had learned that it was in fact almost impossible to rebuild a modern toaster from its basic elements. Moreover, even if it was possible, it wasn't desirable to do so—the sheer effort and waste involved made it unsupportable. What he did learn, however, beyond an appreciation for the technology in even so lowly an item as a common kitchen appliance, was how global production had become and how reliant humanity had become on processes that were arcane even to the experts.

On a philosophical level, his efforts had run into the problem exposed by Zeno's Paradox. It was impossible to define a starting point for the project. No matter how far back one went to get to the basics, there was another level beyond that. He concluded with a marvelous quote from

Carl Sagan: "If you wish to make an apple pie from scratch, you must first invent the universe."

The teacher assigned the students a short thinking exercise to consider Sagan's words, and then discuss how it applied to the UnHappy Meal. What did they now think were the project's goals?

Student 1: "This quote really . . . opened my eyes up to our burger project. We aren't truly going to make a burger from scratch but we are going to come as close as possible. We can't make an earth and make the process of how things grow, so we aren't really starting from scratch. To me this takes away a burden on my shoulders of making the burger perfect. We will be making a burger that is not perfect but successful."

Student 2: "Our goal of this project and the mind webs we made and the paperclip assignment all revolved around the idea of starting at the absolute beginning. In all the projects we looked at where things originated and how they are made. Our, or at least my own, conclusion is there really is no absolute beginning. So therefore we can see that the Burger Project can never be a success, but we are attempting to get as close to perfect as possible."

Student 3: "I mean, no one can really create anything from scratch because everything comes from everything. (Does that make sense?) And, it also ties into our Burger Project at a much more simple note. We cannot recreate the universe, this is true. But, some of us may have to purchase some salt or some other hard-to-synthesize ingredient. This project is about sustainability, but if we can't make a certain something, I think that just helps our understanding of the impossibility of the task we are undertaking."

So, if the meal itself was not the yardstick for success with this project, what was? Perhaps it was an appreciation for just how hard it is for humans to feed themselves sustainably and locally. The impossibility of the project provided a tangible window into just how deranged many of the aspects of the American lifestyle were. If the students became experts into why the project couldn't work and the lessons about the food industry, they had learned from that, then the UnHappy Meal could go back to being what Thwaites had suggested it was—"a bit of showmanship to lure in the audience."

The teacher went back to that very first project the kids had done—the how-to video. It had required the students to present themselves as experts, and to think about the best way to teach someone else what they knew. It made sense to come full circle and have the students become experts in one topic and make a speech that cast them as experts on food.

Each student developed a "Big Idea" that was the germ for their Expert Speech, as this assignment was called. The research for this final speech would be the last major investigation of the school year. As the day for the communal meal approached, they were tasked with organizing notes from their research, drafting a storyboard for their presentation, and adding audio-visual components using the very same rubric we had created for that very first project in September.

The students' range of ideas was impressive—they covered a host of topics from the respective carbon footprints of industrially versus locally raised produce to the nature of capitalism itself. This had been one of the goals of the project, to give students the space to find topics they cared deeply about, and then to give them the time, space, and motivation to become activists.

Neil had chosen to examine whether it was possible to feed society by raising the standard of care and treatment for livestock, and if not, could it be done without recourse to meat at all.

Andrea wanted to make a container that was a comment on the thing contained—a bag made out of cow manure to package cow meat—as a way to illustrate her talk about the transgressive nature of advertising.

Based on her fears the Earth was running out of room, Cady was investigating how to use new kinds of spaces—the sea, the cities, underground—to grow our food. In a similar vein, Lorrie was concerned with the lack of healthy food choices in the inner cities and how urban dwellers could find access to better alternatives.

Katherine and Paul were taking more metaphysical stances in their writing. Katherine was comparing the social milieux of the United States and France to see if the culture of eating had an effect on health. Paul was wondering if the kind of food people ate could move them up or down Maslow's hierarchy of needs.

Isaiah and Donnie were treating fast food craving as an addictive disease. Donnie was reading about studies conducted on rats and concluded that the lack of nourishment from low quality food actually reduced people's motivation to seek out healthier options. Isaiah discussed whether dieters should use methods used by drug addicts to change their behaviors.

Tilly was still pursuing the world of food additives but had changed her focus somewhat to the degree with which it would ever be possible to know what was in industrially prepared food.

In a related issue, Jason wanted to know if and how corporations could be induced to change their practices. Was legislation the most effective way, or moral persuasion, or was it best to appeal to the bottom line and use the profit motive to shift America's agribusiness leaders.

Jack and Natalya were both horrified by the conditions under which meat chickens were raised, while Kyle was horrified by the toll their entire meat was taking on the environment. Cal was horrified at the skyrocketing rates of obesity among children, due partly to fast food.

These speeches would ultimately be filmed rather than be delivered live, but it made sense as they were not the performance. They would exist as artist statements accompanying the true performance—the meal itself.

DEVELOPING A PERSONAL VISION FOR SUCCESS

Part of the theory of handing the students the wheel was that they would not only choose their own destinations, but they would have to become responsible for assessing themselves along the way. Could they understand why they had chosen the path that they had? Could they figure out how to regain a sense of direction when they got lost? Finally, and perhaps most important, would they know when they had arrived at their destinations? Could they motivate themselves to keep persevering until they got there?

The Dunning-Kruger effect is a fun theory that gets a lot of traction for people trying to show why organizations don't succeed well. It is a real phenomenon developed by a college professor of psychology and his graduate student, who wanted to assess how well their students thought they had performed on tests versus how well they actually did. The short of it is that higher performing students thought they had done a poorer job than they actually did, and the reverse was true of the lower performing students, whose confidence outshone their abilities.

From this, Dunning and Kruger concluded that smart people exaggerated the intelligence of the people around them, while incompetent are simply too incompetent to gauge their abilities correctly. The first few episodes of *American Idol* and other competitive reality shows are driven by this phenomenon.

Teachers wrestle with this problem constantly, even if they don't recognize it. Many teachers can recall that it is often the A students who seem hungriest for feedback and who are the quickest to re-edit their work, even when they don't need to. Is that because they are grade-grubbers, or because they underestimate their own abilities and assume they are doing worse than they actually are?

On the other side of the coin, there are the students who never apply feedback to their work, who don't bother reading comments, who seem content to get the same grades assignment after assignment, or who constantly offer wrong answers in class. Is it an unwillingness to apply oneself, or just misplaced confidence? If students lack the critical capacity to understand they aren't high achievers, how does one help them improve? Don't they have to recognize that they are not in fact models of excellence first in order to be willing to correct their work?

A repeated activity throughout the year for these ninth graders was peer critique. It was a way for students to learn how to work together effectively and to see each other as resources. It was also a way to give students several new sets of eyes for their work. Finally, it furnished opportunities for students see examples of mastery for comparison to their own work. Peer critique can raise the bar for the whole class.

But again, if a student does not know enough to see that he or she needs to improve, can they understand what an "A" really looks like? They may become excellent rubric creators, or even excellent peer critics, but that still doesn't necessarily mean they can apply these standards to their own work. The notion of an audience, explored in chapter 8, can have a mobilizing effect on student work, but is there a process the teacher can use in the classroom to get past this hurdle?

By February, the ninth graders had done enough rounds of peer critique and self-evaluation that several students saw marked improvements in their writing. The Dunning-Kruger study concluded that repetitive exposure to examples of excellence would in fact do the trick if a teacher kept at it long enough. Yet, it is difficult to prove that they wouldn't have improved as much if the teacher hadn't just told them what to change and how to change it. If one perceives school simply as a series of summative assessments, there probably wouldn't be any difference in the results between peer and teacher feedback.

If one views education as a process, however, it becomes hard not to imagine that if students develop the critical faculties to see how to make their work better on their own, despite how painfully slowly it seems to happen, then that might transfer over to other spheres. Formative assessment seems to be the key to transference. It gives students an awareness of how they are learning—what's working and what isn't—and they can apply it to different subjects, in sports, in guitar lessons, wherever they seek to improve.

The "Feedback Feedback" exercise had helped quite a bit with the students' writing. It would be interesting to try it again, but this time in a more social milieu. It would test the notion of transference, but also whether the students were willing to view their social habits with the same criticality as they did their schoolwork.

Two problem areas that have wreaked ruin on class projects are work ethic and team collaboration. Some students genuinely have no interest in trying hard at school, especially if they have no buy-in whatsoever to what is being learned. Yet other students who actually seem motivated still struggle with putting forth their best effort or working well in project teams. A useful test of the value of formative assessment, of process thinking, would be if the students could accurately self-diagnose not their academic output, but their affect and behaviors.

Mr. Werberger's Teacher Journal

I have always feared that I didn't really know how to teach collaboration or self-assessment in an effective, replicable way. In the past, it has
seemed to me as though some kids just eventually, magically, come
together and produce work independent of all my attempts to teach
them to work together, and some kids just never pick it up—at least not
in the ninth grade. I was beginning to think it was perhaps develop-
mental, just like physical maturity.

On the other hand, given that this is an experimental year, I have become used to making my own thinking visible to the kids and throw-
ing my own challenges back at them to see how they respond. I think
it's valuable to show the students that I fail at times, that I still have to
problem solve my way through challenges. I wanted to see if they
could talk about workmanship and collaboration at the level of my
own thinking. And I wanted to see if they had any good ideas that we
could adopt as practice.

I wanted to present this as a problem that needed solving. I told them
that I had created a number of pass/fail benchmark assignments that
netted many students consistently mid to high "A'"s all year if they
were simply completed.

I don't feel bad about that, since the kids had told me the work has
been hard enough to keep them challenged. But I felt that we'd never
really had a discussion about what an A or a B or a C really means,
outside of the rubrics we create to assess particular assignments. Therefore, I had noticed an often wide divide between their self-assessments
and the assessments by their peers.

I wrote three words on the board—"okay," "good," and "great," and
asked them what these words meant in general.

For "okay," the students decided it meant just useful enough to pass,
but not worthy of special notice. The work would do, but it was what
would be the last chosen when everything else of value had been snaffled up. Or it meant the work was marred by mistakes—not enough to
make it unusable, but enough to make it unattractive or undesirable.

"Good," was, well, good. No mistakes; competent; useful. They struggled with coming up with more until I asked them what it was like to
be a good athlete, or a good doctor. Good meant that the team might
win, and that the doctor would save you, but you wouldn't be so
impressed that you wouldn't shop around for another quarterback or
another doctor. Good athletes had skills, but didn't necessarily step up
to be leaders or do things impressively. They did not dominate. They
did not beat other players so much as let other players beat themselves.
They were just good enough not to lose.

I changed the word "good" to "proficient" on the rubric we were making.

That led us to "great"—a word they argued with, some wanting it to
read "exceptional" instead to stress the fact that not everyone can get
there (in other words, if everyone is great, great isn't that great after
all). Regardless, they agreed that this category meant that something

inspiring had been created, something extra creative, something
unique (something that other educators would call "beautiful"—
worthy of sharing or saving). As with the word "good," I changed
"great" to "mastery."

I asked them—where do you place yourself in this continuum in terms
of the effort you put out, or the way you interact with your team? They
were to evaluate themselves on this rubric and try to provide examples
where space was provided in order to justify the rating. I instructed
them to take this self-assessment and tuck it away in their folders for
later. I didn't need to see it, as this was a practice run (and I added this
to encourage them to be honest in their self-assessments).

Then I handed out a fresh rubric and told them to evaluate the members of their Unhappy Meal team by their efforts and their teamwork
along the same "okay-to-mastery" continuum. These I did collect, and I
told them that that evening they would receive their teammates' evaluation in addition to my own, and they had to write a reflection in
response to these prompts:

- Compare how your peers and I evaluated you to your own self-
  evaluation. If there are differences, how do you account for them?
- Can you provide examples, if not in this class, where you've hit
  mastery?
- Which sorts of behaviors will you adopt to make your group and
  yourself succeed, whether it's for this project or other activities in
  this class?

For my formal evaluations, I tried to be as honest as I could about what
I had seen, telling some students that they appeared passive and disinterested during group work, or consistently did less than they could
on written work. Or that they actively distracted their peers and foiled
forward progress. I kept in mind that these were ninth graders, but I
also felt that if they couldn't take constructive criticism at this point,
after six months of successive peer critique, then that entire process had
been a failure.

I was pleased with what I read from their reflections. I especially liked
the moments when the students had to confront the sometimes wide
gulf between their own estimations of themselves and those they
learned from me and their peers. What I wanted to see was whether
they could adapt the peer critique and self-assessment of their written
work and apply it to their behaviors.

Student 1: "My self-reflection was more positive than my teacher's was.
I had written that I had a mastery in cooperation, although, after reading my teacher's comments I realize that I am borderline proficient. I
have not been listening to others and applying what they have said to
my work. I can get swept up in the idea I am having at the moment and
can have trouble accepting redirection and suggestions. I do not always
have the motivation to take that extra step toward a more thorough job.

I also need to work at not just listening to what others say and continuing on my own ideas, but internalizing their suggestions and using them."

Student 2: "My peers assessed me at a mostly proficient standard. For me to advance to mastery, I will work out more of the prices and budget for the things we will need to order (seeds, lights, planters, etc.). I will take count of the things we have and the things we need. If we already have some price ideas, I will look into it and tally it up. I'll see if I can find better deals and things along those lines.
Getting feedback helped me snap myself back into a productive space. In class, I will try to be more of a leader. I feel like the ideas that I do give are valuable, I just need to stay productive, which I'm planning to do."

Student 3: "I was a bit surprised. Why had someone put my name under Mastery in Leadership? I didn't think of myself as a good leader. I mean, I got people to stay focused for a good minute and a half once, but that's about it. When I do something helpful, I usually go off and do it myself and then come back with the result; I like people, but when I have an idea I just want them to go away. And I suffer, like most members of my group, from the belief that I have the best ideas.
"We've all gotten good marks and praise for our work in the past, so we figure we should be able to do this project real well and real easy. Problem is, we haven't yet agreed on what 'real well' is. We have different ideas about what this project is for and how it should be done, and we think if we just keep going with our own idea, other people will eventually follow along. But that doesn't happen, and we get some conflicts. And anyone outside of the conflict just kind of feels uncomfortable and doesn't do much about it, so as you can imagine, we could be getting a lot more done without these conflicts."

Student 4: "Which sort of behaviors will I adopt? Well for starters, patience, as it is key to everything. With time and patience our group could be hardworking and use our time efficiently. Patience is something I individually need but also something that would work best if the whole group was actually trying.
I also need to adapt leadership skills, although I feel as if leadership is in my blood and I generally generate the new ideas and keep my group members on track, it seems to be as I was assessed other members didn't feel the same way. So maybe I see leadership potential in myself, but I need to act upon it so we can continue the group in a new direction."

Artists seek to know the world just as historians and scientists do. Unlike historians and scientists, artists are also seeking to know themselves. These two quests are intertwined. The act of learning changes the learner and their relationship to the world. As T. S. Eliot wrote in *Four Quartets* (1943),

> We shall not cease from exploration
> and the end of all our exploring
> will be to arrive where we started
> and know the place for the first time.

Just as with any other epistemology, art begins with questions and goals. Those questions may be simply about the means of communicating, they may be existential, or they may be, as arts-based research suggests, an inquiry into the workings of the physical universe. Art, again, may be unique in that it actively encourages the researcher to avoid making objective statements in favor of a more formative subjectivity. Art asks the maker, "How am I changing myself by this act of experimentation?"

In that regard, an arts-based approach may be the most effective strategy for enabling students to achieve metacognition and see themselves as a proper subject of study. To come full circle from the beginning of the chapter, it links the hand to the brain and adds the further benefit of introspection and self-awareness, or soul. It is no wonder that some of the most highly esteemed scientists in the world are also practicing artists. Art adds personal meaning to the search for knowledge.

This ninth grade class had begun in late August with as a set of socially fragmented and mentally scattered post-eighth graders. By April, they were becoming formidably mature and focused young adults. Part of that was simply biological maturity, but their thinking was evolving. They were becoming holistic thinkers, able to find connections between disparate ideas; they were becoming entrepreneurs who were now used to solving challenges with flexibility; they were becoming activists who were finding their voices.

The last step was for them to become actual artists, and create an exhibit of their work.

NOTES

1. Janinka Greenwood, "Arts-Based Research: Weaving Magic and Meaning," *International Journal of Education & the Arts* 13, interlude 1 (2012), www.ijea.org/v13i1/.

2. William McNeill, "Mythistory, or Truth, Myth, History, and Historians," *American Historical Review* 91, no. 1 (February 1986): 1–10, www.historians.org/about-aha-and-membership/aha-history-and-archives/presidential-addresses/william-h-mcneill.

EIGHT

The Exhibit

The UnHappy Meal Project could easily have been framed within a food ecology course, or a survey on human geography. Growing lettuce and raising chickens could have been construed as fun "hands-on" activities designed to carry students along through the drier parts of a seminar on farming. Labeling it an "art project" and making it the center of the class created a new approach to learning itself.

To develop "artistic sight," the students had been training themselves to look deeply into things—whether in a picture, in an article, or in a cheeseburger—and take pains not to overlook even the most familiar details. They had been instructed to question what they actually knew about everyday items or beliefs, and even to wonder why they didn't know as much as they thought they did. In the case of the Happy Meal, they speculated how else it could exist—which new forms it could take, which new ingredients it could contain.

As arts-based researchers, they had developed strategies to answer their questions. They learned to use each other as critical audiences, resources for feedback to strengthen their work, or as resources for real-time problem solving. They embraced the swerves that their investigations threw at them as opportunities for refining their questions. They had blurred the lines between observer and participant by actively reflecting on how they were learning, and how their experiences were changing them.

The final step, as the end of the project drew near, was to consider how their work should be shown. As individual artists, they had to consider their own pieces, their own artifacts—for the Organics team, were they going to offer a folded bag of homemade paper, or a sack stitched together from leaves and twigs (as BeBe initially wanted)? What could the vegetable team show to make their point about locally sourced food or organic farming? Did the Meat and Dairy crew want to show a deconstructed chicken, or show a graphic depiction of an industrial slaughterhouse?

However, the greater problem, as was soon revealed, was how to show all these pieces together. To do that, the students would also have to become curators. They were going to have to put on a show. This became the most conceptually difficult part of the project. It also became the most rewarding—by curating, the students' own understanding of how much they had learned from the year became clear.

CURATING IS CREATING

> Curating an exhibition of artwork requires editing and "picking things out," yes–as an art museum curator, you're searching your own museum's collection for what would be appropriate for the idea of your show, and you also search other museums and private collections for supplementary pieces. But curating in a museum also requires research, idea development and refinement, project management, budget management, programming considerations, educational training, decisiveness, and even interior decorating skills.— Chelsea Emelie Kelly, "What Does It Mean To 'Curate?'" [1]

Curating does not mean arranging trifolds around a room, like in a science fair. If the sole object of a student exhibit is to statically display knowledge, then that may suffice. Curating assumes that there is a greater purpose to work than simply showing facts on a display board. In fact, the first step to curating is to discover that purpose. What is it that the audience should understand? Only from that can the proper location be identified, or the relationship of the individual pieces to each other conceptualized. Only then can the *hard* work begin of curating begin.

The students were woefully unprepared for this step. They had become used to talking about their progress, both within the context of the project, but also as ninth grade students. According to their parents, they weren't talking about much else when they went home during school breaks. They had had to restate their purpose and their role in the project for each adult they worked with, and for the reporter from the *Chatham Courier* who had come out to interview them. By now, it should have become routinized.

Moreover, they had each compiled a portfolio of their first semester work for the winter finals. They had chosen five artifacts that best illustrated their challenges and successes, and written an essay that identified how far they had come as learners and how far remained to go before summer. By now, many of the ninth graders could talk about how their writing had improved, how their critiques were getting more analytical, or of the breakthrough that had enabled them to create a thicker ink. If anything, they were getting a little overly confident. This was resolved in early April by a small public meltdown.

Mr. Werberger's Teacher Journal

The ninth grade students were asked to present on our UnHappy Meal to the entire faculty and students for about fifteen minutes during the third quarter Academic Awards Ceremony. We did not have much class time to prepare, so I presented this challenge to the kids and we batted around some ideas for how to proceed. They thought it made sense to talk about their most meaningful individual experiences rather than try to summarize the whole project in a short amount of time. They thought it would be more interesting to the audience that way. I ended up with ten volunteers.

On the day of the presentation, I told the students to be careful and not read their speeches right off the page. To a person, they said, "What speech?" One student actually had a piece of paper in his hand, but he folded it up and put it in his pocket and said, "I changed my mind at the last second about what I want to say. Is that okay?" Apparently, they felt confident they could speak extemporaneously about this project, that they could just "wing it."

Alas, they found quickly they could not. One by one they stood up in front of the crowd, brimming with energy and passion which slowly dissipated as they found they could not articulate just what they were learning from the project. It didn't fit neatly into answers or sound bites. They were grasping at larger truths but lacked the vocabulary to express them. They stumbled and meandered through their narratives. One student visibly sweated through his shirt as he desperately tried to bring his story to some meaningful conclusion. As each student finished, they sat down abashed and tried to avoid each other's eyes.

I felt bad for them, but I was also worried that we hadn't put our best foot forward. I imagined people saying to each other—"What, they spent nine months growing tomato plants? How is that 'history'"? I agonized over this for a few days, but it was the headmaster who pointed out that the kids had at least gotten a taste of what presenting was like and had learned they couldn't wing it on the actual exhibit day, and that as far as being authentic went, that they had each found a passion for learning that couldn't be denied.

So, if I viewed this as a first attempt at presentation, I found I was really thinking about the answer to a basic problem that I was myself struggling with—how to summarize eight months of a learning process that was inherently ad hoc and process-based, and which didn't really have an "end." The students hadn't yet had the opportunity or the time to develop that big picture understanding with all the research and physical work they were doing for the physical components of the meals. Moreover, our prospective audience was thinking solely of the creation of food as the end in itself.

This became clear in the context of an article that appeared in the *Chatham Courier* about the project. The reporter seemed engaged in the project, but his initial questions to the kids were on the order of—"how has this changed your eating habits?"[2] After some discussion, he began to see the real question was "how has this changed your thinking habits?" But it took a longer discussion with him to reach that insight, and that was time the students wouldn't be allotted on the day of the actual presentation.

The students had, by this point in the year, four weeks to design a public exhibition that condensed nine months of learning—of research investigations, of habits of mind, of community interactions, of self-reflections and practical farming—into a forty-five minute performance that included a full lunch service. I needed help just starting the conversation, much less dreaming up a plan we could actually carry out.

ART AND SOCIAL PRACTICE

My question to myself as an artist has always been, "How do I make something that engages my city—that creates art where people don't expect to find to it? And how can we change what's valued and how we value it?

—Swoon

By this point in April, the students had already begun to construct their Big Speeches—that is, a two to three minute speech that would present them as experts on one particular topic. It would not be effective, however, to simply blast one speech after another at the audience. Would anyone understand why they were receiving these lectures, or would it be another repetition of that Awards Ceremony performance? What linked all the students' work together—something more than making food—and of what use was all this effort?

Therefore, a way to assist the students might be to transition their questioning process from "what do I know," to "what do I want other people to know, and why?" By thinking explicitly about the *consequences* of their work, the students would become educators, not just content providers. This is an aspect of the arts that holds the most opportunities for teachers looking to engage students with issue-driven topics—a nice mix of individual self-expression with social intervention. This is "social practice."

Tom Finkelpearl, the director of the Queens Museum in New York, defines social practice as "art that's socially engaged, where the social interaction is at some level the art."[3] An example would be the work of Mel Chin, who founded Operation Paydirt in 2006 as a way to focus national attention on lead-contaminated soils in poor neighborhoods. Chin was concerned about the effect of lead poisoning on the children of

New Orleans, and suggested the link between youth violence and learning disabilities as a result of environmental toxicity. The problem is that would cost the city 300 million dollars to clean the soil.

Chin organized an exhibit in partnership with school children, who were asked to create 100-dollar bills called "fundreds" as a symbolic fundraiser. He transformed an old house into a "bank vault" to store the fundreds until they could be delivered to Congress. The effort spread nationally, which required other cities to develop their own vaults and pallets to display the Fundreds that had been created by local students. To pick up the "money," Chin drove an armored truck to tour the various collection centers. At each stop, the truck became the locus of a school awareness campaign.

On one level, Operation Paydirt can be seen as an exploration into urban planning, and as a nonprofit that links activists with donors and social entrepreneurs. Yet it has also had a transformative effect on the schools that Chin visited. The Charlotte-Mecklenburg school district in North Carolina took the opportunity to launch a multidisciplinary study in environmental poisoning that culminated in an informational video PSA. Researchers and artists continue to develop lesson plans for K-12 schools that blend art, science, and research and fundred pallets appear in various city art museums.

Chin argues that art has a duty to play a transformative role in society. He likens art to a virus that can sneak into a host's body and quietly "infect and infiltrate" its ideas, "coursing through the mucosal highway of human beings"—a phrase he used in a lecture for a performance titled *I See . . . the Insurgent Mechanics of Infection.* His work is part of a trend in which artists spurn galleries and formal museum exhibits in favor of public spaces and calls to action.[4]

Similar collaborations between artists and local communities have sprung up in a number of cities, with activists getting publicity for the reforms they champion, and neighborhoods getting their physical needs met. The artist Swoon is renovating a church in Braddock, Pennsylvania, with ceramic tiles the local residents have made in the kiln she built for them. San Francisco's Victory Garden movement teaches children the value of urban gardening to secure fresh, healthy produce in what is considered a "food desert." Performance, creation, and installation have become inseparable from investigation, organization, and self-help.

What makes this different from simple social activism is the importance of performance. Miranda Lash, curator of modern and contemporary art at the New Orleans Museum of Art, refers to "poeticism"—or, the poet's unique self-expression compounded of metaphor and individual perspective—which she says is something "which we demand in art but that you wouldn't look for in the way a church distributes canned goods."

Because of Swoon's ceramic kiln, the residents of Braddock are working together to restore their old church. Individual self-expression and community reintegration thus go hand in hand. The lesson is to imagine what else the community can collectively create to meet other needs. Art may pack the seats, but it can also cause a profound shift in the minds of the audience in a way that other forms of community action cannot.[5]

This is another way to think about formative assessment—not just to see work as stages of a student's development, but to evaluate each artifact by how much closer it comes to realizing the creator's larger social goals. By thinking specifically of purpose, the students were able to come to some agreement about how to link their individual and collaborative efforts. Their answer to this problem took three parts:

1. The students had been engaged in a yearlong process of *ostranenie*, or defamiliarization, in which they had been instructed to question not the physical world, but their own education.
2. Once they had articulated that, they knew they wanted to awaken the same feeling in their audience. They wanted their guests to realize how little they knew, and how much they didn't actively think about on a day-to-day basis—about food, but also the purpose of knowledge.
3. Finally, they had to figure out what to show, and what to create, to make that possible, and to make sure the UnHappy Meals were the prop, not the focus.

PUTTING IT ALL TOGETHER

The students were given the problem directly the morning after the awards ceremony. They agreed it hadn't gone off so well, and some had gotten negative feedback from peers—"Is that all you guys did this year? Make paper? I did that in third grade," kinds of comments. They agreed that was an unfair question—some of them said they had done more work for this class than for any other, both in time served and in overall output.

They quite rightly pointed out that the purpose of the project needed to be clearer, that it wasn't really just to make a Happy Meal, but was an attempt to understand more of how the world worked through the mechanisms by which humans feed themselves. They had begun to think of their learning in a different way—that they had developed habits of mind and a sense of curiosity that was spilling out into areas of their lives, and they wanted to show that as well. Yet how would an exhibit stress the experimental, often self-directed, occasionally nature of their learning?

By coincidence, the school's art center was featuring work that one of the teachers, Dennis, had created for his MFA. A series of ink washes and mixed media works hung on the walls, along with his artist's statement.

The whole class walked over and was instructed to view the work with two questions in mind: "What do you think this work is trying to explore and which is the final version?"

The students struggled a bit with the first question until they found the artist's statement, but they understood the answer to the second question almost immediately—all of them and none of them were the final version; rather, they were experimentations that together represented the artist's vision (and the answer to his own question.) They understood that the purpose of the exhibit was to show the artist's process—not just the final step. In fact, just showing the last completed painting would have been pointless, as it wasn't comprehensible without the several iterations that preceded it.

The students were led upstairs into a working studio, and Nikki, who had led the Organics crew, gave them a quick tour. Examples of her work, all still in process, hung on the walls or lay on the floor. She had been experimenting with ink washes and powdered concrete, and she explained to the students that her latest efforts were an attempt to purposefully recreate an effect achieved accidentally in an earlier painting. In other words, a chronology of the pieces in her classroom could be read as a series of experiments—a process of learning and creating.

Seeing these physical illustrations of what had been to this point a purely abstract problem opened things up for the students in the ensuing discussion.

Mr. Werberger's Teacher Journal

Back in my own classroom, I asked the students to write down, on Post-it® notes, at least five things they had learned this year. They could be bits of content, skills, or even just realizations. I then placed the students in groups, and asked them to group the comments each student in that group had made by whatever similarities made sense to them.

The second task was to list at least five ways they had showed their learning—in other words, could they come up with five artifacts as evidence of their responses to the first question? What followed was a Gallery Walk so that the students could look at each other's lists and take ideas back with them to add to their own.

They ended up with something like this, which is a more organized version of what the kids actually wrote:

What have I learned?
How to know my teacher.
When my learning is driven by me, I am more involved. Failing isn't a bad thing—it's something you can learn from. How I can be persistent

in something that seems impossible. I learned how to care for a living thing. I learned how to create things myself by hand.

I learned how to study with better techniques. I improved my writing. I learned how to organize my thoughts.

I learned how not to freak out about work. I learned how to organize my time. To write with a purpose, not just to take up space. How to write informally with ease. I learned how to see, think, and wonder. I learned how to find good websites.

I learned how to work with others. Your peers are just as helpful as your teachers. Never blow off someone who's trying to help you. I learned how to adapt to others' critiques. I have learned how to work in a group—even an "awful" one. I have learned to communicate with people I normally don't talk to. I have learned how to teach people, and use video.

I learned thinking outside the box. Have a different way of looking at things—you can understand things better by looking at them from different angles. The teacher is not always right. How to stop and think about a completely different approach. How to rise to a challenge in a more creative way.

History isn't Napoleon Bonaparte finding the Rosetta Stone, it's the stone's impact on the world. You don't need to read out of the textbook to understand history. I learned that history is not all black and white. I learned that to understand history we have to think in a creative way. School is not a game of follow the leader. Technology's progression isn't a straight timeline—it's kind of like a tree.

I learned not everything has a simple answer. I learned to look at more than just the facts. We don't know where things origins are. I can't look around me and point out a single thing's original location. I learned that people including myself are really dependent on others. The common man probably doesn't have or know the skills to make a sandwich from scratch.

The Europeans were terrible people in the nineteenth century. I learned about imperialism in the Congo and East Africa. I learned about the pros and cons of American capitalism. I learned about both sides of imperialism. I learned that imperialism can destroy a country's culture for generations afterward.

I learned about poverty in New York.

I learned how to raise a chicken. How to hold the chicken. How to muck out a chicken stall. I learned responsibility for the chickens. I learned how to make paper myself. I learned how to grow cucumbers, tomatoes, and lettuce. I am learning how to make cheese. I've learned how difficult it is to make a Happy Meal.

I learned about food ethics in different parts of the world. I learned about how fast food chains work and what we consider fast food. I have learned about CAFOs. I have learned that corporations can be pretty good or just as bad as I thought they were. Food is as complicated as a toaster, etc.

How have I learned them?

- Going to McDonald's
- Critique
- Discussion and argument
- Studying imperialism
- Debate
- Essay
- Studying the Congo
- Blog posts
- Art and history
- Dissection
- Mind mapping
- Raising chickens
- Planting food
- Happiness research blog
- Studying how much families eat
- Making comments
- Analyzing documents
- Reflecting
- Teaching
- Making a video
- Self-reflections
- Using pictures to document progress
- Portfolio
- Self-assessments
- Thinking Routines
- Reading dossiers
- Burger schematic, etc.

This was particularly gratifying for me to see—I had spent so much of my teacher career invested in using summative assessments to measure student learning, and being often disappointed. This was far richer than I'd hoped for, and while each student had found things of value in their individual explorations, they had collectively agreed on a number of the skills and habits of mind they had developed in common. The list was also longer than they had envisioned—which I hoped was a pleasant surprise.

Each section of the class then engaged in a brainstorming session to com up with overarching ideas to link these statements and artifacts togethe into a collective whole. They created lists of these ideas and tacked ther up on the walls. The ideas were often interesting, but too numerous t winnow down by means of a conversation.

Instead, the constraints—the short amount of presentation time allo ted them, the fact that only a month remained to plan the exhibit, tha they had several other classes to worry about—were listed on the boar

and the students walked around the room "marking" up to three suggestions that they liked that fit within the parameters of what was possible.

Out of that activity emerged the following statement, which was
emailed to every student the next day:

> Dear Class;
>
> Here are the results of your voting. Our theme is: What does this pro-
> ject tell us about ourselves, how we live as a society (our values, our
> expectations, the consequences), and as individuals (how you learn,
> what you think is important to understand, what you want the world
> to be)?
>
> Our plan is to have a different station for each component of the pro-
> ject, side-by-side with the same component from McDonald's. That
> means, our chicken nugget versus theirs, our packaging versus theirs.
> We will have an explanation of where each component comes from—
> both ours and McDonald's. We can have information like infographics,
> pictures, videos, factlets, and so on, at each station.
>
> However, we are using food as a symbol or metaphor or departure
> point to reflect on some different questions. We are not just showing
> people how to make cheese, but why it matters to make it. It's not just
> how to grow vegetables, but why it may matter where it comes from or
> how it's grown. For example, what do these two ways of getting food
> say about the values that we have, or how our society is organized?
>
> So the second part of this exhibit will illustrate what it means to do a
> project like this, to talk about the things that we value in our education,
> that are important to us, and how we learn—not what we learn. We
> will discuss things like: learning a real world situation, dissecting and
> deconstructing objects, self-reflection, doing research, discussing and
> writing.
>
> It's important to note that there was no universal or common response,
> that we are following our own desires and educating ourselves. We
> want to talk about how we can live and be happy in the future.
>
> One idea that has come up time and again is collecting the work you
> have created that has value and displaying it—whether as a timeline,
> or a collage. I think that is fine but it has to be organized and placed in
> a space ahead of time that people can see, and there has to be a state-
> ment made that explains it.
>
> So, Part 2 is for each of you to go through your blogs and Google Docs
> and select your best work—essays, project updates, research blogs,
> self-reflections, art constructions. Part of our class days will be spent
> figuring out how to exhibit this body to the school, and how we want
> to summarize it.

In other words, there were now three multi-media parts to this exhibit
that each student was expected to contribute to:

- A short speech that showed their ability to present on a specific
  issue—to speak like an expert.

- A contribution to the food display that illustrated the physical act of making—a record of how they learned to grow or raise and create an artifact related to the Happy Meal. This was meant to be a classroom exercise for the next three weeks, as it was inherently collaborative even though each student had his or her own piece to work on.
- A contribution to the gallery of work that exhibited their epistemological growth in all types of thinking skills—or, the written artifacts that showed the evolution of their academic learning. While each student would add something to the collective body of knowledge, only a few students would work on it in a form of curatorship.

Though the students were understandably nervous about the exhibit, not a single one had argued against doing it. They had come to understand, as many artists do, that the work isn't finished until it has an audience.

THE IMPORTANCE OF SHOWING WORK

Art is a form of communication. You might think you make art as a form of self-expression, but you know that your work is incomplete until people see it and respond to it. You understand the synergy that erupts when you are in a room full of people looking at and talking about your art.

— Alyson Stanfield, the Art Biz Blog

The idea that student work should be exhibited is not a new one. Science fairs and school literary journals have seemingly existed as long as schools themselves. Plays, musicals, recitals, dance concerts provide a sort of rhythm throughout the year for kids, parents, and teachers to come together every few months for performances.

Some schools, such as High Tech High, have created celebrations of learning, a sort of carnival of academics in which projects in the various disciplines can be displayed or even demonstrated—as in a mock casino in which guests play games that illustrate the mechanics of probability.

Proponents of what are called "authentic audiences" for schools suggest that overall student achievement rises when it is understood that their work will engage the public. Learning matters more when someone might actually use the results of that effort. Students will take pride in work that is well received by more than the teacher. Expeditionary Learning, which partners with schools across the United States to promote community-based projects, shows on its website evidence that reading and math scores rise significantly when student work has a public focus.

John Hattie, a professor and researcher of education in Australia, quantified a number of different factors that affect student success or failure, and released his now famous "Hattie Rankings" in 2009. The list, which exists on his website, *Visible Learning*, places "reciprocal teaching" as the third most effective student-based approach for the classroom, behind self-reporting grades and Piagetian learning. In other words, mastery plus communication is a recipe for high achievement.

Artists have a corresponding purpose for exhibiting their work. Beyond the similar sense of accomplishment that comes from finalizing a project, they are also communicating the fruits of their exploration to an audience. However, that audience is expected to communicate back. Art is in that sense a dialogue between creator and receiver. A state of play exists around the piece, whether it is a static object—a painting, a poem, a photograph—or a live performance.

The audience can even add meaning to the piece by reinterpreting it, or in the case of Marina Abramovic's 2010 "The Artist Is Present," becoming part of the performance itself. Abramović sat in a chair at her own retrospective show and invited museumgoers at the Museum of Modern Art to sit silently across from her and gaze back. The only variable that changed, in fact, was the participant. In contrast to the artist, who remained impassive, many of the sitters lost control of their emotions, and their portraits may be seen in a blog titled "Marina Abramović Made Me Cry."

The UnHappy Meal exhibit was therefore a blend of scholastic and artistic performance. It was literally meant to be consumed, passively, and actively. The audience would receive knowledge about the source of their food, and then they would eat it. The students wanted to create the same sense of defamiliarization in the audience that they themselves experienced throughout the course of the project.

Regardless of their success in actually creating a replica of a Happy Meal for display, the exhibit was really their final assessment. In order to achieve their didactic purpose, they had to carry out a series of related tasks that encompass the work of a curator—they had to manage a series of tasks, from building the actual artifacts and designing their physical layout, to developing artist statements, advertising the show, installing the pieces, and creating a sense of drama and theater for the show.

Therefore, space had to be given during the academic week in order to plan the event. The two sections of ninth graders were combined for a day to facilitate a nice, long discussion. Each of the three production crews was handed some scratch paper and pens, and asked to draw up a schematic of the physical display they wanted to make. As they worked, they were pushed to not just indicate how the paper and ink, or the chicken patties and cheese, would be displayed, but to also write down their Expert Speech topics and any questions they wanted to engage with to evolve a purpose.

The students involved in curating the learning artifacts worked with a visual artist who helped them brainstorm a strategy for showing student work with a specific goal in mind. She asked them searching questions, asking them to think about the space—in this case, the school dining hall—and what assumptions they could make about their audience, who would be their peers and teachers. What would help them understand the message?

The process was slow and argumentative, but after thirty minutes of back and forth, something resembling a consensus approach emerged from each table. The teams were given a much larger sheet of easel paper and asked to create a clean second prototype that would also indicate who was to work on which parts, their "needs and gots" (what they needed versus what they already had) and their schedule for completing the final product from the second prototype.

Oddly enough, the bulk of the students' energy and excitement was reserved for their production crews, rather than the original UnHappy Meal project teams they had self-selected into back in November. As a result, the students agreed producing a complete UnHappy Meal—that is, a burger in a bag, with fries, and a toy—was less important than showing each of those components in detail in separate stations. The old teams were abandoned and the production crews created Google Docs to share their thinking as they met over the next four weeks. The Google Docs were an excellent way to capture the process of problem solving.

Excerpts from the Paper and Ink Team's Planning Document

Jason: What am I doing? Trying to make paper, simply. I'm not doing so much folding and stuff, because I'm mostly just working on making the wrappers/sleeves, which mostly consist of ordinary sheets of paper. I might also explore with ink a bit.

What are some questions that are important to think about with packaging that can make people care about this issue? For instance—why are we trying to make this naturally? Why use sustainable resources? Why recycle? What are major problems that we can explore around packaging?

The paper is from nature, so . . . we reuse old paper to make new paper, which recycles—we can keep making new paper. Because . . . factory process cuts down trees. So, what is someone says, it's only a tree . . . and there's a lot of them . . .

Well, we use paper every single day But it takes a long time to make paper—will we run out of trees?

Do we have proof that we waste paper? Or that we are running out of paper? Could you find proof?

I want to see if we can print some stuff on our paper. That would be impressive.

Cal: I think we could/should make a video of our process in making paper. I think that would be cool.

Andrea:
Big Idea for Paper: Recycling using natural resources (cow manure)
Big Idea for Ink: Advertising and appeal
Toy: Materialism
The reason I used no design on cow manure paper is to put zero emphasis on anything. Gender roles, advertising, materialism, none of it. I am trying to use my part of the project to create the opposite of a McDonald's meal.

Lorrie: We could present our paper/ink by actually just showing it having an art exhibit.
We can do the exhibit on our own paper! Use colorful paper or trifold and put our paper on top of it. We can make a video of us making the paper exactly like we would in hands to work and the bag. Have a SPEECH ready or a few comments on what we are doing? Q AND A? For the hands-on exhibit I think we should have two boxes and the paper we made and a normal sheet of paper you can buy from the store and have people reach in and state which one they think we made. I also like the idea of having a trifold with our paper displayed on it. What I want to present that is so important about our exhibit is that we are making our paper out of ALL recycled materials. Without that we wouldn't be able to make the paper. That's why it is so important to recycle your old boxes or paper. Also I'd like to present how much time and dedication it actually takes to make one simple piece of paper.

BeBe: I do not care about the problem of the paper, or why should I recycle it. My perspective about the packaging and the toy are why McDonald's packaging interests the kids and why parents trust them. Why do they split the toys into boy toys and girl toys?

Kyle: We had such an amazing day yesterday. We shared the works, we talked a lot about this exhibition. So the result is, we are gonna have two different folders. One is about paper wasting and ink making. We are going to make a video next week for the whole process of making paper. Jason, Lorrie, and Andrea are gonna take charge of it. And the other one is about the toy. We are gonna share the reasons why we made these toys. BeBe, Cal, and I are taking care of this.

Lorrie: SO! Presenting! We talked today and we mostly agreed on everything right? Here's what I took from it: we will have a trifold with our paper displayed on it, the ink will be the writing on the trifold so we arent using any materials we haven't made (besides the trifold.) We will then have a laptop or iPad whatever fits next to the trifold which will show a time lapse of how we made the paper. Every one of us who had something to do with the paper/ink will give a brief speech-type thing about why it is so important to us. Then we will have an addi-

tional trifold with the information on the toys with the same materials.
RIGHT?

Jason: Recycling paper is the easiest method for us, as we are working
on a tiny scale and don't need perfectly white and smooth paper.
So, a nondefinitive, incomplete, not-final-in-any-way list of exhibit
components:

- Container of paper pulp—interactive? Let people swish it around?
- Container of ink, and also maybe have the stuff that the ink is made
  out of (whether it be beets or berries or what have you) next to it
  #TransformationTuesday
- Paper sheets (with ink displayed on them somehow, perhaps write
  "McDonald's" or something) to feel and look at
- McDonald's Happy Meal containers and toys for comparison, per-
  haps with short statements about the appeal of ours vs. theirs
- Our toys, with short statements about why we chose the toys we did
- Include some of the infographics, like the one that says the McDo-
  nald's M is more recognized than the cross for Kyle's toy statement
- Blind A/B test—Lorrie
- Interaction is essential—Lorrie, Andrea
- Jason's iPad: Film: How-to Videos on Wednesday

Mr. Werberger's Teacher Journal

In looking over the schematics and planning documents, I could see
that each crew's approach was visibly different, but made sense given
the nature of the components they were working on. Moreover, they
had finally begun to integrate those bigger questions I wanted to see;
how much paper was being wasted in packaging our food, or how the
industrial live stocking industry operated and its effects on the animals
and us, the consumers—and this was being integrated in an aesthetically pleasing and organic way.

As the date of the exhibit neared, the student's workweeks became a
blend of planning days, production days, individual blocks of time dedicated for creating the Expert Speeches, or for peer feedback on the same.
The notion of silo'd class times and daily schedules broke down completely as students gave up their free periods to work in the kitchen, and
postdinner free time in the dorm was used instead for further planning or
meeting with the teacher for extra help.

There were last-minute meltdowns between group members from dis-
agreements about the display to frustrations over perceived inequities of
effort. While the Organics crew worked together very smoothly, some

crews split to form smaller groups, and even teams of one. The Vegetable crew found themselves creating competing displays in order to avoid further arguments.

The Meat and Dairy team fought initially over who would get to present the fun side of chicken ranching—the difference between the lives of their chickens and those in factory farms. The losers in that dispute surrendered gracefully and had to take on the grimmer task of documenting the slaughter, which was also compared to the processing occurring at the professional chicken farms.

The curating time experienced the existential conundrum of planning a labor exhibit from work that hadn't been created out of a common sense of purpose. One idea they had was to assemble student work from the past eight months into six stacks, covering color-coded themes as "research," "hands-on," "reflection," and so on. Each pile would exist at a differently colored table, and each table was tied back to a central table that explained the nature of the mind-web they had created.

One of the students responsible for this display wrote in his blog, "We definitely have a final goal, but I'm just not sure exactly how we want to present. I want people to, as closely as possible, experience our eight-month trek through mud, dirt, snow, books, websites, information, and just general work. I want to find a way to show the journey we actually went through, not just a burger." This color-coded system was their attempt to explain how much else had occurred beyond making a meal.

In order to "sell" the exhibit, they began collecting phrases they liked from student submissions, and pasted them onto paper coded to the colors they had agreed upon for the six learning topics. These were strung from the ceiling in the various school buildings, and a statement of purpose hung in the library. The phrases they chose were not only designed to explain the coming exhibit, but also to impart a feeling of strangeness and a bit of unease in the reader—to provoke and evoke.

Student Excerpts

"We dissected a chicken that had died not long ago . . . it was gross and oddly fun."

"I'm going to try and blend cow crap and newspaper to see what happens."

"How do you feel about having your tomato plants growing in your bathroom?"

"If we can somehow get the rest of my stupid, fat, lazy, Internet addicted generation to be curious and to be heard, the world may change greatly, and all because she didn't like the chicken nuggets."

"Seeing how things really work was all too important to pass up, as we explored what small things we helped create the bigger image, it planted this seedling of an idea of what learning reals is, and what we actually do in schools."

"I think I now know how to be awesome at stuff, I just have to work on it a little bit."

"My group truly believed that our point was validated and the only correct point. Sadly, so did the other group."

"After the dissection, Mr. Werberger asked if the project was going to ruin our lunch meal or not. I was determined to eat."

"Four weeks of taking care of chicks is like four weeks of taking care of twenty-six children that eat you out of the house and won't shut up. The resemblance to teenagers can be shocking."

"I have discovered that the chicks enjoy listening to Swedish rap music, indie pop, and Angsty alternative rock. So my entire Spotify playlist."

"Fingers crossed that I don't check on the lettuce tomorrow and they're all dead. That would suck."

One of the members of the Curating team, Isaiah, tried to address head-on the dilemma of whether students or faculty members casually drifting by the various tables would actually take the time to read longer examples of student work. Many of the research blogs were several pages long. His thought was to turn these mixtures of investigations, reflections, essays, and critiques into a work of art.

He had been taken by the work of two faculty members of the arts department, who had used ink washes to create unexpected effects in their paintings. He took every piece of student writing, laid them out in a row on the lawn, and poured a mixture of ink and water over them from a sprinkler can. Then he tossed handfuls of dirt on them to give them a granular appearance. They took two days to dry.

This act of spontaneous experimentation wasn't appreciated by the other members, Cady and Johann, who hadn't been consulted, and they formed their own duo while Isaiah tried independently to figure out what to do with the ink-splattered pages. The twosome now decided that they would place fresh copies of student work on the dining tables while the color-coded central tables would now be littered with the quotes that had formerly hung from the ceilings of the various buildings on campus, and on each table would sit a laptop queued to a video playlist of the expert speeches.

There were also small surprises, such as when the paper and ink team ran a page of their cow manure paper through the printer—the paper emerged safely on the other side, reading "Dear God, please don't let this get stuck."

Every student participated in some way to help prepare the food. The Meat and Dairy crew made farmer's cheese the week before, but the rest of the duties were shared the two or three days before the exhibit opened. That meant making the buns, the condiments, and grinding the chicken into patties on Monday, and peeling turnips and parsnips for fries on Tuesday. Everything else would be cooked on Wednesday morning. An ancient cider press was dragooned into use to make the beverages.

Mr. Werberger's Teacher Journal

I stood mostly in the middle of the room, helping as needed and haranguing the few kids who were trying to sneak off and get on their phones. It was fewer than I had expected, actually. It was a fascinating thing to watch—the creation of a show that I had had little directly to do with planning or executing. "Awesome" might be a better word, actually. The students assumed almost total control, needing my help only with off-campus tasks such as getting a few Happy Meals for comparative purposes.

I heard one of the students exclaim, "I've never been so stressed and so happy at the same time!" This was probably the best thing I would hear all day—this was the good stress that comes from wanting to do a good job for the sake of the thing itself. A win for our team!

At the last moment I realized we needed emcees, and I corralled the curators to handle the job of introducing the exhibit's purpose to the students and adults who began to file into the dining hall at 11:00. At that point, the presentation took on a familiar sight—of students explaining the information on their displays in greater detail, and engaging in some attempts at social activism.

At 11:30, the doors to the feed line opened, and tables were sent up two at a time to get their lunch. When I saw the first loaded plate emerge, I almost cried. On each of these big, gorgeous rolls sat a chicken patty on a bed of lettuce from our own garden, topped with farmer's cheese made by our hands and locally sourced ingredients, with a side of parsnip fries and condiments made from scratch.

What of the ink-splatter experiment? I copy below the curator's own words, taken from an accounting I asked of each student of how they had contributed to the exhibit.

Isaiah: Over the past weeks I have assisted Peter and Cassidy in creating the idea of hanging papers and helped organize the larger presentation. . . . Eventually we got to the point where we were basically done and I decided to go off on a tangent. I took the stack of essays and blog posts from which the quotes were extracted . . . and reconstructed them. I honestly had no clue what I was doing or why I was doing it.

About ten minutes before the presentation I was blanking on creativity. I had placed the dried blackened papers on a solid white table. It was not pleasing and there was no color. So based on the recommendation of Mr. Werberger, I overlaid the essays on colored schematics for the UnHappy Meal. I quickly, with five minutes remaining, in a state of panic, wrote an artist statement and asked people to please interact with papers however they see fit. Some students ripped the paper. Others moved the papers to see the underlying schematics.

At one point I actually ended up promoting Donnie's paper and took it out of the pile and offered it to teachers to read. The article was well written and connected [physical and emotional] abuse to history, which I find absolutely amazing . . .
I had no clue still why I did such a thing with the ink, but I knew I was trying to make a statement. I ended up switching my "why's" [several times], but my most favorite answers were spurred by the viewer, such as "the ink formed a lens, a lens of a student's thoughts on a teacher's idea." The schematics were pretty basic and tight to how the teacher presented the project and the overlaying essays were reflections. I came to the conclusion that this showed how everything is a perception, what one person sees another may see totally differently.

It seemed fitting, somehow, that the display meant to summarize student learning was completely improvisational and based entirely on audience interaction to provide that meaning. It was in itself a microcosm of the UnHappy Meal project—a long-term experiment in a different kind of learning that promised a high degree of critical rigor, deeper practice of academic skills, *and* greater individual freedom for the students than any other project in the teacher's fifteen years of experience.

If this was an experiment, it did beg the question—How could it be determined if the project had been successful?

NOTES

1. Milwaukee Art Museum Blog (http://blog.mam.org/2012/06/15/what-does-it-mean-to-curate/) posted June 15, 2012, accessed July 21, 2015
2. Vince Pecoraro, "'Unhappy Meals': Darrow Ninth-Graders Deconstruct, Reconstruct McDonald's Happy Meal," *Chatham Courier*, April 8, 2015, www.columbiagreenemedia.com/chatham_courier/news/article_93552e60-dd6f-11e4-a7ca-779f9908ed82.html.
3. Pecoraro, "'Unhappy Meals.'"
4. Carol Strickland, "Getting the Lead Out: Mel Chin," *Art in America Magazine*, April 1, 2014, www.artinamericamagazine.com/news-features/interviews/getting-the-lead-out-mel-chin.
5. Strickland, "Getting the Lead Out."

NINE

Measuring Success

The problem with summative assessment has already been discussed — guaranteeing success on tests meant to summarize learning usually means teaching what will be on the test. The students did not learn any formal math or science, some history, a little literature, a grab bag of academic skills, but nothing that is particularly quantifiable. That said, there must be some way to evaluate what happened to the ninth graders in wake of the UnHappy Meal's grand finale.

On the simplest level, one could ask whether the students succeeded in creating the meal. On that score, the answer would be a qualified yes. Food was created, more or less from scratch, and packaging was created from materials at hand. However, the students did not milk a cow for its cheese and then butcher it for meat. Neither did anyone make a soft drink from some chemical process and construct a waxed paper cup to hold it in (or a straw, for that matter.) No one in the audience seemed to mind that was missing.

Yet this was always meant to be an art *experiment*—not an "academic project" (although it was that, and more). They created an artist's palette together—the skills of creative thinking, inquiry, collaboration and communication; the small bits of knowledge that they chose to discover; and the ability to improvise as new problems constantly arose over the eight-month quest. The UnHappy Meal itself was never the most important goal.

Thomas Thwaites got his toaster to work—for thirty seconds. Then it blew up. He was not able to recreate every component from scratch. In the end, he settled for what was possible, and even then it didn't work out as it was intended.

In no way can that be considered a failure. He ended up with a book, a TED Talk, and a guest appearance on the Colbert Report. He came to

145

some essential truths about the nature of industrial production and the average person's alienation from it. He also inspired an equally improbable classroom project.

Some different metrics should therefore be considered for the project's outcomes. First, what are the measurable outcomes, in general, from progressive education? What does it mean to be "ready for college"? In other words, what should students be learning? If standards are subjective, who should be asked what those standards should be, anyway?

ASSESSING PROGRESSIVE EDUCATION

The UnHappy Meal project ranged across a number of approaches. In that it began with a specific artifact as the end goal, it borrowed aspects of project-based learning. However, the students were tasked with a variety of open-ended challenges, including the exhibit; thus, it incorporated elements of design thinking, problem-based thinking, and challenge-based thinking. The inquiry process was a cornerstone of the project—every activity began by workshopping questions prior to an investigation and eventual write up. So, what's in a name?

Regardless, they all have some basic elements in common—and therefore, those elements can be assessed. All these approaches favor open-ended questions with multiple possible answers. Students are expected to take the lead in solving these problems—they figure out what they need to know and develop strategies to fill the gaps. During this process teachers forego lecturing or otherwise directing the students, instead "leading from behind." Finally, projects tend to be practical, applicable to the "real world," and multidisciplinary.[1]

These characteristics implode standard testing models, and make quantification imprecise. Educational researchers have had to create new standards for measuring the effectiveness of these student-centered pedagogies. Woie Hung suggests assessing students' meta-cognitive faculties by evaluating the depth of their research into a topic, their research methodology, their ability to apply "logic and effective reasoning," and their ability to solve problems. Finally, have they learned the content knowledge appropriate to their investigation, and how to use it correctly?

Doctors Brigid Barron and Linda Darling-Hammond at Stanford break down the process of research by evaluating the student's ability to use evidence accurately in support of an assertion, to weigh competing opinions, and to write clearly and persuasively. They also suggest that a student's ability to work well and profitably with others is a key indicator of learning and growth. Both studies use the same criteria to judge instructional design. In other words, a good project incorporates these skills, and a good teacher knows how to facilitate them.[2]

Curiously, when it comes to preparing students for traditional, content-based exams, progressive educational models actually do no worse than traditional techniques, and in many cases, students coming from PBL or design-thinking classrooms do better than their peers. Therefore, some research suggests that some of the additional outcomes for students are increased self-confidence and motivation (or, emotional intelligence) and an ability to apply knowledge from one venue to another. Again, these more internal outcomes are hard to measure, and as a result, seem to come largely from student self-reporting.[3]

Colleges are beginning to see the benefits of PBL and its cousins. Some of the first studies of hands-on problem-solving pedagogies were done in medical schools, and following suit, some engineering programs are beginning to incorporate more design-thinking challenges for freshman and sophomore level courses.

An article in *U.S. News & World Report* suggests that dwindling enrollments in engineering are caused by the traditional lecture- and content-based courses that have little practical connection to student's lives. Harvey Mudd College now gives entering freshmen the task of deconstructing a pencil sharpener and explaining how it works.[4]

Some experts are rethinking the notion of college readiness. In addition to knowing basic content knowledge, University of Oregon professor (and CEO of the Educational Policy Improvement Center) David Conley claims that students need to "think . . . act, and go." Thinking means "problem solving strategies, conducting research, interpreting results, and constructing quality work products." To act requires "ownership of learning, and learning techniques such as time management, note taking, memorizing, strategic reading, and collaborative learning."

To go, students need an awareness of what is available for them after school, and how to get it. This includes self-knowledge and advocacy. Finally, knowledge does matter, but Conley places as much emphasis on a student's "willingness to expend effort to get it," and a student's understanding of an academic discipline's structure and epistemology, or knowing how new knowledge fits into what is already known.[5]

Frustratingly, the same studies that show the gains made by student in PBL and related classrooms also suggest that teachers still struggle with some of its basic methods:

[O]ne study found the following barriers to successful implementation of PBL: (a) projects were time-consuming, (b) classrooms felt disorderly, (c) teachers could not control the flow of information, (d) it was difficult to balance giving students independence and providing them supports, (e) it was difficult to incorporate technology as a cognitive tool, and (f) authentic assessments were hard to design.

Teachers also may struggle with entrenched beliefs when attempting to implement PBL. For example, it may be challenging to negotiate between giving students opportunities to explore their interests or covering the state standards, allowing students to develop individual answers or providing students with one correct answer, and empowering students to direct their learning or controlling the distribution of expert knowledge.[6]

Therefore, it is possible to evaluate the UnHappy Meal's success, and its usefulness, by these criteria—both by what was gained and what was avoided.

ASSESSING THE UNHAPPY MEAL AS AN EDUCATION

The students wrote at least one research investigation every three weeks, and each time followed a careful pattern of using thinking routines to extract details and develop investigative questions. They assessed the usefulness of their resources, weighed competing points of view, and wrote multiple drafts in response to their questions. They used rubrics to guide their writing, and collaborated in frequent peer critiques to improve their work. Frequent reflective writing assignments required them to self-report on their progress.

They were required to develop holistic thinking skills over the year. They deconstructed objects to understand how the parts worked together, and how they could be rebuilt differently. They had to understand the global food system by looking at its different components—and furthermore, to understand their own place within it as a consumer. They had to assemble an exhibit out of a dizzying number of artifacts and points of view, as well as assemble a lunch for 150 people.

They had to design authentic products and plan their way through several stages to completion by a firm deadline. They had to combine aspects of several different disciplines to be successful. They had to be creative and adaptive, seeking out a variety of resources after identifying needs that seemed to switch from day to day. Sometimes they had to get up early or leave the dorm late at night to feed chickens because someone forgot a shift.

They analyzed several different forms of writing—novels, primary sources, journal articles, newspapers, and websites. They wrote quite a bit on their own—research blogs, essays, project narratives, self-reflections, and peer feedback. They practiced different forms of note-taking: annotations, T-charts, and mindwebs. At different points in the year, they self-diagnosed their progress with these skills.

Their teachers, whether directly connected to the project or in other disciplines, all noted growth in these areas. A more pertinent question is whether the students themselves noticed their growth, whether in these more quantifiable categories or in those of emotional intelligence, motivation, time management, or confidence. The students were asked to write a self-reflection the day after the exhibit and discuss how they felt for tenth grade. Several excerpts are included here:

Student 1: "When I first started the year off I had no clue how I should act or behave and that definitely showed in my first quarter. I just didn't have any motivation at my old school so I didn't really care if I got a C. But in Werberger's class I started to become more enthusiastic in the learning process. I started to do my research better and put more time into my essays because I wanted to do well and not screw up. And at the end of the second quarter I think it showed that I had grown and started to care more about my grades. I put a lot of time into writing my blog posts and writing my essays."

Student 2: "Even though I did not really learn much history during the course, I really began to learn about myself. Through this class, it began to become clear that I work better in a casual learning environment. It was nice to be able to work at my own pace and really focus on what I wanted to. I really feel like I matured as a person during this class, and I want to thank you for that.
"Originally, my past years in school I have believed that working in groups was easier, since the work was distributed between everyone. I always thought that I could get away with not doing any work. In this class I found out that working in smaller groups, of like two or three, made a really safe and nice learning environment for me. I even found that working by myself was enjoyable and that I could do it successful-ly. . . . This class helped me learn that I could work in a group and actually get work done by myself and not depend on everyone else to do everything."

Student 3: "I understood that independent learning is. . . . You guessed it, independent. When I understood that I would only get as much back as I put in I took control over my education. Many people in our class understood that and I think the quality of work we did improved expo-nentially throughout the year."

Student 4: "I am a very hands-on learner and I comprehend informa-tion more by applying it to things, and this class was very hands-on — especially with the burger project. One thing that helped me a lot was all of the learning methods that we [used] such as mind maps, schemat-ics, and the thinking exercises which have helped me organize my thoughts."

Student 5: "[A]nother thing this project provided that a conventional lesson couldn't: actually having to work with people for a goal that mattered. I mean, group projects are a standard thing, but this was different because people were graded individually as well as having a group grade–this kept everybody pulling their weight most of the time,

and is more like an actual work environment in that you are responsible for something and can face consequences if you don't do it. So
yes, more time would have been even better, but everything is hard
until someone makes it easy.

"I feel that this project, and the class in general, has prepared me for
that kind of work, work that matters. . . . My writing has improved, my
time management has improved, my perspective has improved as well
as my ability to work with people; and while it's great that I learned
about the Congo, too, I think it's much more important that I have
these skills, as the ability to do things is what will carry me through life
much more than knowing things. Knowing that "2+2=4" won't help if
you balk at "3+4=?".

Student 6: "I'm shocked that in the last midterm I struggled to write
two pages and now I am flying through it like it's no problem. I liked
how you taught us about structured essays more than I had learned in
any of my English classes. I especially loved the Tumblr blog updates—
continue to do that! It helped me with my writing and made me enjoy
it rather than dread it."

One of the parents had been particularly curious about the project and
wrote a note after the year was over to identify some of the changes she
had seen in her son.

In the past (as a student in our public middle school), he would do
exactly what was expected to maintain A's in his classes. No less, but
certainly no more. Very rarely would he take on extra work or explore
questions beyond the confines of what was assigned. I didn't get the
impression that he thought much about what he was studying in
school beyond the hours spent either in the classroom or completing
homework. He definitely felt that much of what was assigned was
disconnected, pointless, or simply busy work. (I have to admit, I had to
agree with him on the homework front much of the time.)

This year has been a whole different experience, especially during the
second half of the year and most strikingly during the final quarter. He
is engaged in the curriculum and with the learning process. (This has
been true for social studies all along, but I also noticed a shift in terms
of his approach and thoughts regarding his other classes as well.)

He clearly is thinking about his courses beyond the classroom and in
the context of and in relation to the rest of the world and his life. It
seems to me that there's been a shift from a compartmentalized approach to school and the rest of his life to one that has lots of blurry
edges and gooey bits where things from the various parts overlap and
come together.

From the February break onward, he would light up and share
thoughtful and insightful tidbits regarding curriculum, assignments,
and how he felt about the work that he was doing. I was particularly
impressed by his meta-cognitive assessments—his ideas about how dif-

ferent activities were more or less successful in his learning process and any adjustments he made as a result.

The actual assignment (i.e., grow tomatoes) was just the springboard. Typically, the actual factoid or specific task would be left behind as he described process, thought, critique, adjustment, and bigger picture considerations. It was clear to me that this represented a lot of thought over longer periods of time on his part than what he was simply tasked to do during class or homework hours.

When we talked about his plans for the summer on the drive home yesterday, he included things he wanted to read, a screenplay that he's planning to write, a desire to visit the Saratoga Battlefield as part of some research he had done regarding Benedict Arnold this past year along with plans to get together with friends, visit family, and catch up on sleep. I think this self-driven desire to continue learning, on his own time, for his own reasons is the very best testament to what a PBL approach can do for students.

Were any of the pitfalls of PBL avoided? Was there a tendency toward disorganization, or unclear projects goals? Was there a tension between student freedom and teacher control? Was collaboration problematic? Did motivation ebb over time? Were there odd rhythms of overwork and underwork, times when nothing happened and times when too much happened? Well, yes. All of these problems occurred from time to time. What is more interesting is how these problems were managed. In general, the default setting was to turn the problem back onto the students.

Hence, the students developed their own investigations, and their own standards for reporting their discoveries. They used their own technology, though they were required to maintain a blog and to use the teacher's own organizational web tool for ease of communication. They worked collaboratively to their own different individual ends, and created their own collaborative groupings. They had a hand in designing their own assessments, and created their benchmarks, often in collaboration with experts. They ignored state standards, and adopted their own standards of success.

Some degree of disorganization—or at least what the students perceived as disorganization—was therefore required for them to have the freedom to invent their own programs of study. Again, the UnHappy Meal was not the ultimate goal. Nor were the research blogs. The goal was to recreate the basic way people learn—before they are taught how to do so in schools. The goal was to have them come to a fuller sense of themselves within the world. The search would help them define themselves. The goal, therefore, was art. How should the project be assessed as an *artistic* experiment?

ASSESSING THE UNHAPPY MEAL AS ART

What are the standards of success for a work of art? What do artists want to happen once the performance or exhibit takes place? How do they evaluate a piece of music, a photograph, a dance, an intervention?

Much as with more formal academic projects, one metric is whether the piece was successfully completed. Beyond that, there is an emotional component that is often missing with more objectively scored work. Musically, what is the difference between playing someone else's composition objectively well—note for note, beat for beat—and playing it in a way that *feels* good. Art is an attempt to communicate a personal vision. Without that sense of authenticity and individuality, that performance might conceivably be rendered as formal practice at best, kitsch at worst.

Art is, after all, an attempt to express an individual concern. It is an exploration in the name of meaning, both of the object being rendered and the artist's position toward that object. Life being an ongoing frame of reference, and the world being infinite, that exploration never ends. So, a different way of framing the idea of success might be accomplishing one's goals as set forth at the beginning, but also embracing room for new surprises and celebrating those new discoveries.

Shaun McNiff identifies the existential nature of artistic inquiry as one where the outcome cannot be known.

> As contrasted to scientific methods, you generally know little about the end of an artistic experiment when you are at the beginning. In the creative process, the most meaningful insights often come by surprise, unexpectedly, and even against the will of the creator. The artist may have a sense or intuition of what might be discovered or of what is needed, and in some cases even a conviction, but the defining aspect of knowing through art . . . is the emanation of meaning through the process of creative expression.[7]

Again, the open-ended nature of the UnHappy Meal—what might be perceived by its lack of a fixed final product and the improvisational nature of its design and construction as "disorganization"—is the critical space necessary for the students to stumble across the unexpected, to make giant leaps of divergent thoughts and pursue their own strange visions. It's the sudden weirdness in the familiar—*ostranenie*, which is to make the banal strange through art—that drives the sort of long-term curiosity necessary to sustain a long project.

Elliot Eisner wrote "education is a process of learning how to become the architect of your own experience and therefore learning how to create yourself. The arts have distinctive contributions to make to that end through their emphasis on the expression of individuality and through the exercise and development of the imaginative capacities." Because the world is learned through the senses, interpreted with the rational mind, but imbued with imagination and personal creativity when meaning is communicated, he believed that the arts should be front and center in schools, not an addendum to them.[8]

Ergo, one should consider an additional measure of success for the project—did the students come to "create themselves"? Did they come to new realizations about the mundane? Did they pursue divergent thoughts and develop a critical ethics about the world? Or did they wander about in a fog for the duration of the school year?

Student 1: "If you ask most people, they will tell you that they have total free will over their choices. But what if that's not the case? How can I show them that well, advertising, and materialism has gotten to them, and how they can free themselves. One problem. I don't know how they can free themselves. Maybe that's the point then. Give them a choice. If they want to lead a life of materialism, let them. Or they could choose not to.

"Look at Siddhartha. He lived a materialistic life for many years, until he finally freed himself at the river. Well, I can show people that they can find their river, be free, or continue lying to themselves and eating up everything McDonald's and every other corporation shoves at them.

"If I learned one thing from this whole project, it's that you can tell people all you want about something, but if they don't want to listen, they're not gonna. So I can show them, show them that there is a life beyond consumerism and materialism. But no matter what, it's up to each person to find that life. To find the initiative to free themselves. I can only introduce the idea. They have to live it."

Student 2: "This year has been incredible. I have learned more life lessons than actual history and I am okay with that. We remade a Happy Meal from scratch—we even killed chickens. This year went well for me at least mainly because there was no set destination. It was mainly student-led, and our final project was completely thought up by the students. That is the way I like to learn—give the students responsibility. Let them choose how they like to learn, let them find a new approach to tasks.

"The year is over and I wish that this teaching style could carry over to my next classes but I realize if I want that teaching style I have it exhibit it in myself. This is going to sound corny, but this class has opened my eyes to examine the world in a whole new light—to actually care about what I eat and what I do. Being able to step back and examine the world and how humanity effects it is crazy."

Student 3: "During this past year, I have learned to accept that failure at a task is not failure of the entire project. I have watched plants that I had put a lot of work into die from frost, I've watched my ideas pulled apart by logic, and I watched possibilities becoming impossibilities.

Through all of this procrastination, laziness, and last minute doing I still see this project as complete.
"[Y]ou still have to remember the burger was never the main concept. The burger was a metaphor for something we constantly have around us and overlook in its production."

Student 4: "I had many questions when I first started this project. This project took eight months—what is the point of using eight months of class and extra time to work on this, to work on a thing that already exists? In the first semester, nothing came together, everything we made failed. The paper we made could not fold, and oil would go through. The ink we made was too light, the color wouldn't show on the paper. I can't make the toy, because I don't know how to make plastic.
"But . . . the guy who tried to make the toaster, his final work was horrible looking. It didn't even toast bread. But he tried very hard to make a thing that already exists—why? I think it is more important to put your own work in the project. Some people may think it is trash, it is nothing. [T]he purpose, your purpose of making it is important. To tell people your idea by showing this single project."

Student 5: "As a final statement, I think I'm really more happy with how I learn things. I don't know if there's a definitive idea that I can put on what I'm doing different, but I just don't think about pieces of technology the same. There's nothing I could create from scratch, there just isn't. I don't know whether that's terrifying, or very very cool."

Student 6: "The chickens are dead. Bummer, right? I mean, It's really hard to think about what went down that Wednesday. These chickens, while given a life that allowed them to lead more healthy, happy, and generally fruitful lives, were killed by our hands. I cut their skulls from their spines, and only after I had raised them. I cried afterward. I cried a lot. The weird thing, though, is that I wasn't 'sad' per se.
"For them to be dead means that we can live, and that is a really neat thing. From their carcasses we got a grand total of seventy pounds of meat and twenty gallons of stock. We are able to live and breath and dance and do whatever we so please because these chickens had, at one point of time, been alive. I have a respect for the animals that gave their lives. I am now a much more conscious carnivore. I am glad that I was able to really see what happens with my food.
"Too many people I know happily guzzle chicken fries and feast upon bacon, but when they are even presented with the concept of animals dying for them to clog their arteries with bacon, they run away from the thought. They try to shut me up and tell me how its so disgusting. They benefit from a creature's death, and never even stop to respect the creature.
"I pray that I never, ever achieve a state of blissful/willful ignorance. It is disrespectful and shallow. Death happens. Deal with it. If you are an

omnivore, I highly recommend trying to witness or participate in a slaughter. Frankly, if the idea of an animal dying to be on your plate makes you queasy, you should be a vegetarian."

HOW ABOUT THE AUDIENCE?

If art is a form of communication, perhaps the audience needs to be included in the evaluation, as well. An artist's statement will fall flat if no one can receive the message. An artist's work can be deepened or even transformed in dialogue with the viewer. Some artists may even prefer condemnation to silence—fury signifies that at least a message was received.

Tracy Emin's notorious 1999 installation "My Bed," a reconstitution of her younger self's bedroom, with its collection of "vodka bottles, [cigarette] butts, used condoms, contraceptives, blood, vomit and tears" below the titular unmade bed outraged thousands of viewers, one of whom supposedly attempted to clean it up and throw away her trash. More recently, two Chinese student-activists jumped into it while it was on display and engaged in a pillow fight in order to respond to it with their own critique.[9]

Did the UnHappy Meal therefore have an effect on the people who came to view it, to hear the student's stories, play with paper batter, and eat the chickens they raised and killed? Unfortunately, that metric is a bit harder to uncover. A short questionnaire sent out publicly revealed that nearly every respondent learned at least something new about the food industry, most of which was disturbing. Some were stunned by how fresh and savory this locally sourced food was compared to the commercially produced stuff. Others keyed in on the excitement and passion, and pride, the ninth graders displayed during their presentation.

There were a few consequences of the project that were not anticipated, but which indicate that some sort of transformative effect did occur.

THE AFTERMATH

Darrow School has made a conscious decision to embrace the design thinking and project-based approach begun by the UnHappy Meal. Future iterations of the ninth grade and perhaps the tenth will find their core classes linked together into multidisciplinary blocks, and will be tasked with making authentic products for the local community. Juniors and seniors will slowly be tasked with creating capstone projects—opportunities to carry out individual inquiry-based explorations in tandem with local experts. Curriculum plans are already in the works.

I have been promoted to dean of faculty, and while I continue in my role as the ninth-grade history teacher, I will also be facilitating conversations across the entire curriculum to find ways of giving students more and more opportunities to have similar experiences as this first cohort. Neither of these two outcomes was planned—both were entirely improvisational.

I am still stunned this project happened. It was an idle speculation that developed from a haphazard conversation with a few artists I had just met. I had wanted to address some dissatisfactions I had with education in general. Now matter how inventive my ideas were, how well I followed all the rules for PBL, it still all felt fake somehow—that I was still putting a box around what the kids could be doing, would rather be doing.

I had hated nearly every day of school after third grade. What I taught myself, from reading and playing around after school, I still remember. Middle and high school? Not so much. It wasn't until graduate school that I began to love learning—it was holistic, it was self-directed, it was collegial. What was I doing still replicating an educational system that I didn't benefit from instead of the one that had ultimately worked for me? I decided to throw caution to the wind and construct an open challenge that eliminated all the barriers to freedom that

I gambled that opportunities would arise throughout the year, and by not having a concrete path or predicated goal, we would be able to take advantage of them in ways that might have been foreclosed by a more deterministic process. To take one example, I hadn't planned on raising chickens for meat—the possibility hadn't even arisen until the second semester—but that led to the most profound engagement with learning I have ever experienced. I also teared up when I watched the chickens die, and I had a hard time taking that first bite of the chicken burger, but I have a vastly different relationship with food now as a result.

There are a number of things I would do differently, of course. I am armed with a better sense of curatorship, and I am already thinking of ways to make that more inherent in the curriculum. The students' writing needs to be made more public still. I will be adopting more of a design thinking approach, which means the challenges will not come from me, but from the kids' interactions with people in the community, and what they learn about local needs. But I am committed to the idea that arts-based research and the artistic process yields the greatest outcomes for the kids.

There were frustrations, of course, and emotional outbursts, and late work, but in truth I have never enjoyed myself so much in the classroom as I did this year. Every student was a character—it was though their academic freedom that left them freer to express themselves as they are. All the discussions about process, all the help problem solving was balanced by their sheer creativity and insight. They had perhaps the fastest route to maturity of any ninth-grade class I've had.

I cannot say this approach will always work, but something unusual happened with this class. I cannot offer a specific list of techniques that you should follow to recreate this, just the tools that made it possible. The nature of art is that something new and unexpected should always happen. Just remember what it was like to learn in kindergarten, and the right move will inevitably follow.

It's your turn to improvise.

NOTES

1. Andrew Walker and Heather Leary, "A Problem Based Learning Meta Analysis: Differences Across Problem Types, Implementation Types, Disciplines, and Assessment Levels," *Interdisciplinary Journal of Problem-Based Learning* 3, no. 1 (Spring 2009), doi: http://dx.doi.org/10.7771/1541-5015.1061.

2. Vanessa Vega, "Project-Based Learning Research Review: Evidence-Based Components of Success," *Edutopia,* December 3, 2012, www.edutopia.org/pbl-research-evidence-based-components.

3. Walker and Leary, "A Problem Based Learning Meta Analysis"; "Summary of Research on Project-Based Learning," Center of Excellence in Leadership of Learning, University of Indianapolis, June 2009, http://cell.uindy.edu/docs/PBL%20research%20summary.pdf.

4. Margaret Loftus, "College Engineering Programs Focus on Hands-on Learning," *U.S. News & World Report*, September 30, 2013, www.usnews.com/education/best-colleges/articles/2013/09/30/college-engineering-programs-focus-on-hands-on-learning.

5. Tom Vander Ark, "Q&A: David Conley on College & Career Readiness," Getting Smart, June 20, 2012, gettingsmart.com/2012/06/qa-david-conley-college-career-readiness/.

6. "Summary of Research on Project-Based Learning."

7. McNiff, "Arts Based Research," 40.

8. Elliot Eisner, *The Arts and the Creation of Mind* (New Haven: Yale University Press, 2002), 24.

9. Alison Cole, "Tracey Emin's 'My Bed' at Tate Britain, Review: In the Flesh, Its Frankness Is Still Arresting," *Independent,* March 30, 2015, www.independents.xyz/arts-entertainment/art/reviews/tracey-emins-my-bed-at-tate-britain-review-in-the-flesh-its-frankness-is-still-arresting-10144882.html.

About the Author

Raleigh Werberger has been teaching history for fifteen years in the United States and internationally. He taught both Advanced Placement and International Baccalaureate classes and over time began to question the entire premise of high school education. His interest in creating authentic experiences for students led him to experiment with PBL and design thinking challenges.

He co-founded a project-based exploratory program at Mid-Pacific Institute in Hawai'i, and served as a founding board member for the School for Examining Essential Questions of Sustainability in Honolulu in 2012–2013. He moved to New York after spending a year with his wife, a photographer and filmmaker, at Akademie Schloss Solitude in Stuttgart, Germany.

He is now dean of faculty at Darrow School in the Berkshires in upstate New York.